A Gift For

_____

From

_____

STRENGTH *for the* SOUL *from* OUR DAILY BREAD

Peace

Discovery House Publishers

Books, music, and videos that feed the soul with the Word of God

Box 3566 Grand Rapids, MI 49501

Introduction

Since April 1956, millions of readers around the world have found daily inspiration, hope, comfort, and biblical truth from the pages of *Our Daily Bread*. Now you can find encouragement from one of the most beloved devotionals on the subject of peace, compiled into one convenient volume.

We believe that this book will be of help to you and those you know in every circumstance of life. May it and the Word of God bring strength to your soul.

Other books in the Strength for the Soul from
Our Daily Bread series

Grief
Prayer
Trust
Comfort
Hope

Load Limit

Now these things occurred as examples to keep us from setting our hearts on evil things as they did. Do not be idolaters, as some of them were; as it is written: "The people sat down to eat and drink and got up to indulge in pagan revelry." We should not commit sexual immorality, as some of them did—and in one day twenty-three thousand of them died. We should not test the Lord, as some of them did—and were killed by snakes. And do not grumble, as some of them did—and were killed by the destroying angel.

These things happened to them as examples and were written down as warnings for us, on whom the fulfillment of the ages has come. So, if you think you are standing firm, be careful that you don't fall! No temptation has seized you except what is common to man. And God is faithful; he will not let you be tempted beyond what you can bear. But when you are tempted, he will also provide a way out so that you can stand up under it.

—1 CORINTHIANS 10:6–13

We've all seen load-limit signs on highways, bridges, and elevators. Knowing that too much strain can cause severe damage or complete collapse, engineers determine the exact amount of stress that various materials can safely endure. Posted warnings tell us not to exceed the maximum load.

Human beings also have their load limits, which vary from person to person. Some people, for example, can bear the pressure of trial and temptation better than others; yet everyone has a breaking point and can take only so much.

At times, circumstances and people seem to be pushing us beyond what we can bear. But the Lord knows our limitations and never allows any difficulties to enter our lives that exceed our strength and ability to endure. This is especially true when we're enticed by sin. According to 1 Corinthians 10:13, "God is faithful, he will not let you be tempted beyond what you can bear."

So when trials and temptations press down on you, take courage. Remember, your heavenly Father knows the limits of your ability to stand up under life's pressures. Draw on His strength; no temptation will ever be greater than that.

—David McCasland

Finding Rest

The LORD is my shepherd, I shall not be in want.
    He makes me lie down in green pastures,
he leads me beside quiet waters,
    he restores my soul.
He guides me in paths of righteousness
    for his name's sake.
Even though I walk
    through the valley of the shadow of death,
I will fear no evil,
    for you are with me;
your rod and your staff,
    they comfort me.
You prepare a table before me
    in the presence of my enemies.
You anoint my head with oil;
    my cup overflows.
Surely goodness and love will follow me
    all the days of my life,
and I will dwell in the house of the LORD
    forever.

—PSALM 23

According to a survey conducted by an insurance company, one of every six workers in the United States feels too busy to take all the vacation days he or she has earned. Even though studies show that a week's holiday each year can dramatically reduce stress and the risk of heart attack, many people just keep working.

A vacation can be good for body and soul. But many people don't have the luxury of time away from work and daily responsibilities. What can we do when we must remain in demanding circumstances?

Psalm 23 paints a beautiful word picture of a caring shepherd, secure sheep, and a tranquil scene of quiet meadows and still waters. But it is the Lord, our Shepherd, who gives rest, not the green grass or the flowing stream. "He restores my soul; He guides me in paths of righteousness for His name's sake" (v. 3).

Rest is a place of peace that our spirits find in God. Neither the presence of those who oppose us nor the dark valley of death can keep us from what hymn writer Cleland McAfee called "a place of quiet rest, near to the heart of God." Through prayer and meditation on His Word, we can commune with Him. In the Lord's presence we can experience the rest and renewal we so desperately need.   —DAVID MCCASLAND

Joy Stealers

Grace and peace to you from God our Father and the Lord Jesus Christ.

I thank my God every time I remember you. In all my prayers for all of you, I always pray with joy because of your partnership in the gospel from the first day until now, being confident of this, that he who began a good work in you will carry it on to completion until the day of Christ Jesus.

It is right for me to feel this way about all of you, since I have you in my heart; for whether I am in chains or defending and confirming the gospel, all of you share in God's grace with me. God can testify how I long for all of you with the affection of Christ Jesus.

And this is my prayer: that your love may abound more and more in knowledge and depth of insight, so that you may be able to discern what is best and may be pure and blameless until the day of Christ, filled with the fruit of righteousness that comes through Jesus Christ—to the glory and praise of God.

—PHILIPPIANS 1:1–11

Why do many Christians fail to experience real joy, which is listed as a fruit of the Holy Spirit in Galatians 5:22?

In his book *Laugh Again*, Charles Swindoll suggests three common "joy stealers"—worry, stress, and fear. He defines worry as "an inordinate anxiety about something that may or may not occur." (And it usually doesn't.) Stress, says the author, is "intense strain over a situation we can't change or control." (But God can.) And fear, according to Swindoll, is a "dreadful uneasiness over danger, evil, or pain." (And it magnifies our problems.)

Swindoll says that to resist these "joy stealers" we must embrace the same confidence that Paul expressed in his letter to the Philippians. After giving thanks for the Philippian believers (1:3–5), the apostle assured them "that He who has begun a good work in you will complete it until the day of Jesus Christ" (v. 6).

Whatever causes you worry, stress, and fear cannot ultimately keep God from continuing His work in you. With this confidence we can begin each day knowing that He is in control. We can leave everything in His hands.

Resist those "joy stealers" by renewing your confidence in God each morning. Then relax and rejoice. —JOANIE YODER

Every Step Counts

When Enoch had lived 65 years, he became the father of Methuselah. And after he became the father of Methuselah, Enoch walked with God 300 years and had other sons and daughters. Altogether, Enoch lived 365 years . . .

The LORD saw how great man's wickedness on the earth had become, and that every inclination of the thoughts of his heart was only evil all the time. The LORD was grieved that he had made man on the earth, and his heart was filled with pain. So the LORD said, "I will wipe mankind, whom I have created, from the face of the earth—men and animals, and creatures that move along the ground, and birds of the air—for I am grieved that I have made them." But Noah found favor in the eyes of the LORD.

This is the account of Noah.

Noah was a righteous man, blameless among the people of his time, and he walked with God.

—GENESIS 5:21–23; 6:5–9

People who want to feel better, reduce stress, and shed unwanted pounds are discovering that walking may be the best exercise of all. A fitness philosophy of ten thousand steps a day, which first took hold in Japan, is gaining popularity in other countries. Experts advise starting slowly and working toward a higher goal, realizing each day that every step counts.

It's even more important to stay spiritually fit by "walking with God," which the Bible describes as an intimate, growing relationship with the Lord. "Enoch walked with God 300 years" (Genesis 5:22). "Noah was a righteous man, perfect in his generations. Noah walked with God" (6:9). Both men are mentioned in Hebrews 11, where they are commended for their faith. "Enoch . . . was commended as one who pleased God" (v. 5). "Noah . . . became heir of the righteousness that comes by faith" (v. 7).

To walk with God, we need to keep in step without running ahead or lagging behind. Along the way we talk with the Lord, listen to Him, and enjoy His presence. We trust His guidance when we cannot see what lies ahead. It is not just the destination that's important, but the journey we take together.

There's no better time than now to begin walking with God, because each day every step counts.

—David McCasland

Sleepless Nights

LORD, you have assigned me my portion and my cup;
*   you have made my lot secure.*
The boundary lines have fallen for me in pleasant places;
*   surely I have a delightful inheritance.*
I will praise the LORD, who counsels me;
*   even at night my heart instructs me.*
I have set the LORD always before me.
*   Because he is at my right hand,*
*   I will not be shaken.*
Therefore my heart is glad and my tongue rejoices;
*   my body also will rest secure,*
because you will not abandon me to the grave,
*   nor will you let your Holy One see decay.*
You have made known to me the path of life;
*   you will fill me with joy in your presence,*
*   with eternal pleasures at your right hand.*

—PSALM 16:5–11

---

*T*he psalmist David had his dark, lonely nights when everything seemed out of control. Doubts and fears assailed him, and there was no escape from his problems. He tossed and turned just as we do, but then he turned to his Shepherd (Psalm 23:1) and reminded himself of the Lord's presence. That brought peace to his anxious, troubled soul. David said, "Because He is at my right hand, I will not be shaken" (16:8).

We too have occasions of wakefulness when anxious thoughts jostle one another for attention, when we curse the darkness, and when we long for sleep. But we mustn't fret, for darkness can be our friend. God is present in it, visiting us, counseling us, instructing us in the night. Perhaps on our beds, as nowhere else, we may hear God's voice. We can listen to His thoughts and meditate on His Word.

We can talk to the Lord about every concern, casting our anxiety on Him (1 Peter 5:7). We can talk about our failures, our conflicts, our challenges, our cares, our frustrations over His lengthy delays—all the things that stress us out and render us sleepless—and listen to what He has to say. That's what can set us apart from ordinary insomniacs. That's the secret of quiet rest.

—DAVID ROPER

Going Home

You, my brothers, were called to be free. But do not use your freedom to indulge the sinful nature; rather, serve one another in love. The entire law is summed up in a single command: "Love your neighbor as yourself." If you keep on biting and devouring each other, watch out or you will be destroyed by each other.

So I say, live by the Spirit, and you will not gratify the desires of the sinful nature. For the sinful nature desires what is contrary to the Spirit, and the Spirit what is contrary to the sinful nature. They are in conflict with each other, so that you do not do what you want. But if you are led by the Spirit, you are not under law.

The acts of the sinful nature are obvious: sexual immorality, impurity and debauchery; idolatry and witchcraft; hatred, discord, jealousy, fits of rage, selfish ambition, dissensions, factions and envy; drunkenness, orgies, and the like. I warn you, as I did before, that those who live like this will not inherit the kingdom of God.

But the fruit of the Spirit is love, joy, peace, patience, kindness, goodness, faithfulness, gentleness and self-control. Against such things there is no law. Those who belong to Christ Jesus have crucified the sinful nature with its passions and desires. Since we live by the Spirit, let us keep in step with the Spirit. Let us not become conceited, provoking and envying each other.

—GALATIANS 5:13–26

*I*n an article for the *Atlanta Journal-Constitution* titled "Hassled for the Holidays," Bill Hendrick describes the tensions of the Christmas season. For millions of people, he writes, "going home for the holidays has become an arduous, stress-filled ordeal in which grown men and women unconsciously revert to childish roles, elderly parents bark orders like tyrants, and somebody else . . . makes all the decisions."

Even in the best of families, holiday reunions can be a stressful time when we experience anything but peace. But Galatians 5 says that as new persons in Christ, we have a choice about our thoughts and actions, no matter where we are. If we live according to our sinful nature, the result is "hatred, discord, jealousy, fits of rage, selfish ambition, dissensions, factions" (v. 20). But if the Holy Spirit controls us, we can show "love, joy, peace, patience, kindness, goodness, faithfulness, gentleness and self-control" (vv. 22–23). When we get together with our families, these Spirit-filled qualities can be seen as we "serve one another in love" (v. 13).

A lot of people are longing for "peace on earth, goodwill toward men" during this holiday season. Let's take it home with us and, by the power of the Holy Spirit, give to family and friends the gift of God's peace.   —DAVID MCCASLAND

A Neglected Remedy

Now Ahab told Jezebel everything Elijah had done and how he had killed all the prophets with the sword. So Jezebel sent a messenger to Elijah to say, "May the gods deal with me, be it ever so severely, if by this time tomorrow I do not make your life like that of one of them."

Elijah was afraid and ran for his life. When he came to Beersheba in Judah, he left his servant there, while he himself went a day's journey into the desert. He came to a broom tree, sat down under it and prayed that he might die. "I have had enough, LORD," he said. "Take my life; I am no better than my ancestors." Then he lay down under the tree and fell asleep.

All at once an angel touched him and said, "Get up and eat." He looked around, and there by his head was a cake of bread baked over hot coals, and a jar of water. He ate and drank and then lay down again.

The angel of the LORD came back a second time and touched him and said, "Get up and eat, for the journey is too much for you." So he got up and ate and drank. Strengthened by that food, he traveled forty days and forty nights until he reached Horeb, the mountain of God. There he went into a cave and spent the night.

—1 KINGS 19:1–9

$\mathcal{I}$ am often asked to speak on the subject of stress. I'm not an expert on stress, just an experienced sufferer! I simply share counsel from God's Word that helps me live less stressfully and more restfully. Many listeners are desperate for any new insight I might offer. What blank looks I sometimes get when I make this particular recommendation: "Get more sleep!" In their longing to deepen their experience of God's peace, they were hoping for something more spiritual than that.

But I'm not alone in linking spirituality to sleep. A godly Bible teacher was asked to share the key ingredient in his own life for walking in the Spirit. He studied the Bible and prayed regularly, but his surprising reply was this: "Get eight hours of sleep each night."

This reply is less surprising in light of God's initial remedy for Elijah's stress and depression (1 Kings 19:1–18). Twice God gave him food and undisturbed sleep before gently confronting him at Mount Horeb with his error.

Psalm 4:8 says, "I will lie down and sleep in peace, for you alone, O LORD, make me dwell in safety." Sleep is not the full remedy for stress, but other solutions can become clearer to people who get adequate rest.   —JOANIE YODER

Anatomy of a Murder

You have heard that it was said to the people long ago, "Do not murder, and anyone who murders will be subject to judgment." But I tell you that anyone who is angry with his brother will be subject to judgment. Again, anyone who says to his brother, "Raca," is answerable to the Sanhedrin. But anyone who says, "You fool!" will be in danger of the fire of hell.

Therefore, if you are offering your gift at the altar and there remember that your brother has something against you, leave your gift there in front of the altar. First go and be reconciled to your brother; then come and offer your gift.

Settle matters quickly with your adversary who is taking you to court. Do it while you are still with him on the way, or he may hand you over to the judge, and the judge may hand you over to the officer, and you may be thrown into prison. I tell you the truth, you will not get out until you have paid the last penny.

—MATTHEW 5:21–26

The newspaper reported a tragic incident of violence that took place in a South American country. A peasant killed his best friend while they were arguing about political differences. When asked why he did it, he replied with these chilling words: "We began peacefully, and then we argued. I killed him when I ran out of words."

This tragedy calls to mind Jesus' teaching in Matthew 5 about the close connection between anger and murder. First He stressed the seriousness of anger (vv. 21–22). He warned that malicious anger, like murder, would be punished by God. Then He gave practical advice designed to defuse anger in a person who has something against another (vv. 23–26).

We should all take a close look at our inner rage. We might think we can control it. Unfortunately, though, our feelings of hostility often control us and cause us to do things we would never do while thinking clearly. That's why unresolved anger needs to be seen as a time bomb that can explode, destroying ourselves and doing irreparable damage to others. True, not all anger is wrong. But all wrong anger needs to be acknowledged and confessed before it leads to "murder." —MART DE HAAN

Grateful for Stress?

When my heart was grieved
and my spirit embittered,
I was senseless and ignorant;
I was a brute beast before you.
Yet I am always with you;
you hold me by my right hand.
You guide me with your counsel,
and afterward you will take me into glory.
Whom have I in heaven but you?
And earth has nothing I desire besides you.
My flesh and my heart may fail,
but God is the strength of my heart
and my portion forever.

—PSALM 73:21–26

In 1812, the genteel New Englander Ann Judson embarked with her husband Adoniram on a long ministry of danger and hardship. The Judsons were sailing to far-off Burma as pioneer missionaries.

Ann recorded in her diary how they survived in next-to-intolerable conditions. "Have been distressed for some days on account of the gloomy prospect before us," she wrote. "Everything respecting our little mission is involved in uncertainty. I find it hard to live by faith, and confide entirely in God when the way is dark before me."

Yet Ann added, "If the way were plain and easy, where would be the room for confidence in God. Instead, then, of murmuring and complaining, let me rejoice and be thankful that my heavenly Father compels me to trust in Him by removing those things on which we are naturally inclined to lean."

Despite extreme hardship, Ann Judson would agree with the psalmist, "God is the strength of my heart and my portion forever" (Psalm 73:26).

What is our attitude when the props we have depended on are suddenly gone? Are we grateful for the trials that can strengthen our faith? For the child of God, great stress can develop great faith—and reveal God's great grace.

—VERNON GROUNDS

Focus!

"Who are you?" they asked.

"Just what I have been claiming all along," Jesus replied. "I have much to say in judgment of you. But he who sent me is reliable, and what I have heard from him I tell the world."

They did not understand that he was telling them about his Father. So Jesus said, "When you have lifted up the Son of Man, then you will know that I am the one I claim to be and that I do nothing on my own but speak just what the Father has taught me. The one who sent me is with me; he has not left me alone, for I always do what pleases him." Even as he spoke, many put their faith in him.

To the Jews who had believed him, Jesus said, "If you hold to my teaching, you are really my disciples. Then you will know the truth, and the truth will set you free." —JOHN 8:25–32

*J*ohn P. Robinson, often called America's "time guru," claims that people today sleep more than they think they do. He says that though they have more leisure time than ever, they still report feeling "stressed, rushed, and crunched for time."

Robinson calls this problem "overchoice." It's caused by the sheer number of options available to fill our time and the wearying realization that no matter what we choose to do, we are leaving something undone. If our identity is defined by activity, we operate on the principle, "The more we do, the more we are." We are exhausted, and we are the reason.

If Jesus hadn't focused on doing His Father's will, He too could have been overwhelmed by all the needy people and demanding tasks He faced. But instead of frenzied activity, Christ personified the focused life in everything He did. He said, "The one who sent me is with me; he has not left me alone, for I always do what pleases Him" (John 8:29).

Each day, Jesus sought to know His Father's will as He moved purposefully to the cross. There, He finished all that God had given Him to do. Today, our heavenly Father invites us to focus on Him for the wisdom and strength to complete the work He has given to us.   —DAVID McCASLAND

Candlelight Wisdom

In the presence of God and of Christ Jesus, who will judge the living and the dead, and in view of his appearing and his kingdom, I give you this charge: Preach the Word; be prepared in season and out of season; correct, rebuke and encourage—with great patience and careful instruction. For the time will come when men will not put up with sound doctrine. Instead, to suit their own desires, they will gather around them a great number of teachers to say what their itching ears want to hear. They will turn their ears away from the truth and turn aside to myths. But you, keep your head in all situations, endure hardship, do the work of an evangelist, discharge all the duties of your ministry.

For I am already being poured out like a drink offering, and the time has come for my departure. I have fought the good fight, I have finished the race, I have kept the faith. Now there is in store for me the crown of righteousness, which the Lord, the righteous Judge, will award to me on that day—and not only to me, but also to all who have longed for his appearing.

—2 Timothy 4:1–8

While traveling in Finland, I learned to appreciate the Finns' lavish use of candles. They never treat them as mere ornaments. Candles bring warmth and light into their homes during short winter days. The Finns know that a candle's purpose is missed unless it is burned. But candles should burn at one end only—a lesson I needed to learn.

When my husband and I began our missionary work, I longed to burn out for God. Within several years I had burned out all right, but not for God. Mine was a classic case of useless burnout, brought on by many self-caused stresses.

One night I hit rock bottom and discovered that the rock was Christ. As He began teaching me dependence on Him for all things, the candle of my life was relighted for His use.

I now see a difference between so-called "Christian burn-out" and "burning out for God." Burnout stems from wastefully burning the candle of our lives at both ends—hardly wise for candles or Christians. Burning out for God means our lives are spent wisely in His service—an echo of Paul's testimony in 2 Corinthians 12:15. Once used up for God, we'll be raised up for heavenly service (Revelation 22:3). It is for this purpose we were made!   —JOANIE YODER

The Unseen Keel

One day Jesus said to his disciples, "Let's go over to the other side of the lake." So they got into a boat and set out. As they sailed, he fell asleep. A squall came down on the lake, so that the boat was being swamped, and they were in great danger.

The disciples went and woke him, saying, "Master, Master, we're going to drown!"

He got up and rebuked the wind and the raging waters; the storm subsided, and all was calm. "Where is your faith?" he asked his disciples.

In fear and amazement they asked one another, "Who is this? He commands even the winds and the water, and they obey him."

—LUKE 8:22–25

The president of Gordon College, R. Judson Carlberg, was driving along the ocean near his home in Massachusetts when he saw two stately seventeenth-century sailing ships. They were replicas that were built for a movie being filmed nearby.

"The breeze was stiff," Carlberg reported, "straining the rigging and the crews. Yet each ship stayed the course and didn't capsize." He explained the secret of their stability. "Beneath the waterline each had a deep, heavy keel—a part you don't see." The keel was essential for keeping the vessel steady in rough weather.

What is it that holds us steady when fierce winds are blowing across life's sea? What keeps us from capsizing when we are under stress and tension? What enables us to sail on, despite the strain? It's the stabilizing keel of faith in our sovereign God. It's our unseen relationship with Christ. As He commanded the wind and the waves on the Sea of Galilee, He also controls the storms and squalls of life that threaten to sink us or drive us off course. Our faith in Christ is an "anchor for the soul" (Hebrews 6:19) that can keep us from ultimate shipwreck.

—VERNON GROUNDS

Interview with a Gerbil

Turn from evil and do good;
  seek peace and pursue it.
The eyes of the LORD are on the righteous
  and his ears are attentive to their cry;
the face of the LORD is against those who do evil,
  to cut off the memory of them from the earth.
The righteous cry out, and the LORD hears them;
  he delivers them from all their troubles.
The LORD is close to the brokenhearted
  and saves those who are crushed in spirit.
A righteous man may have many troubles,
  but the LORD delivers him from them all;
he protects all his bones,
  not one of them will be broken.
Evil will slay the wicked;
  the foes of the righteous will be condemned.
The LORD redeems his servants;
  no one will be condemned who takes refuge in him.

—PSALM 34:14–22

With appealing humor, Ron Hutchcraft, busy author, speaker, and counselor, tells about his battle with stress. One day Ron decided to "interview" the family gerbil.

"Tell me, Gerbie," Ron asked, "what do you have planned for today?"

"First, breakfast," he replied, "and then get started."

"Doing what?" Ron questioned.

"Why, the same thing I did yesterday, and the day before that."

"What's that?" Ron asked again.

"The wheel."

And sure enough, Gerbie climbed on his little wheel and started running in circles. Hours later, he was still running.

The more Ron watched that gerbil, the more he saw himself. He had his own personal "wheels"—demands, deadlines, aggravations, ambitions. He felt as if he were running in circles, and he longed for peace. In his search, he made this discovery in Psalm 34: Peace isn't automatic or passive; it must be pursued. Not only that, but peace is also a result of a right relationship with the Lord.

As never before, Ron enthroned the Lord as the Shepherd of his life. As he did, peace, instead of the stressful wheel, became normal. Which will be normal for you today?

—JOANIE YODER

Burned-out Jugglers

"To whom will you compare me?
*   Or who is my equal?" says the Holy One.*
Lift your eyes and look to the heavens:
*   Who created all these?*
He who brings out the starry host one by one,
*   and calls them each by name.*
Because of his great power and mighty strength,
*   not one of them is missing. . .*
* Do you not know?*
*   Have you not heard?*
*The L*ORD *is the everlasting God,*
*   the Creator of the ends of the earth.*
He will not grow tired or weary,
*   and his understanding no one can fathom.*
He gives strength to the weary
*   and increases the power of the weak.*
Even youths grow tired and weary,
*   and young men stumble and fall;*
*but those who hope in the L*ORD
*   will renew their strength.*
They will soar on wings like eagles;
*   they will run and not grow weary,*
*   they will walk and not be faint.*

—ISAIAH 40:25–26; 28–31

*T*oday's wife, mother, and homemaker is a professional juggler. She balances home, church, and community responsibilities and often runs a family taxi service.

My daughter Tina is a juggler who admits that she sometimes feels like resigning, but she's learned where to go with her struggle. Here's how it began.

One morning Tina woke up with the I-can't-juggle-it-all feeling and started to panic. Reaching for pen and paper, she began recording some spiritual "first aid," such as, "God is not stressed out. God is not frustrated. God is not exhausted. God is not confused. God is not panicking."

After listing what God is not, she began listing what He is: "God is relaxed. God's timing is perfect. God has continuous energy. God is in control. God knows everything." Then she wrote, "This God is living in me. He is working through me." By the time she wrote those words, Tina's panic feelings had flown. Before she had a chance to say, "God, I want to resign," she realized that He wanted to renew her strength.

Are you a juggler needing God's first aid for your soul? Guided by today's Bible reading of Isaiah 40, ponder the Lord's limitless attributes. Then let Him renew you.

—JOANIE YODER

Willing to Change

"Why have we fasted," they say,
    "and you have not seen it?
Why have we humbled ourselves,
    and you have not noticed?"
Yet on the day of your fasting, you do as you please
    and exploit all your workers . . .
Is not this the kind of fasting I have chosen:
to loose the chains of injustice
    and untie the cords of the yoke,
to set the oppressed free
    and break every yoke?
Is it not to share your food with the hungry
and to provide the poor wanderer with shelter—
when you see the naked, to clothe him,
    and not to turn away from your own flesh and blood?
Then your light will break forth like the dawn,
    and your healing will quickly appear;
then your righteousness will go before you,
    and the glory of the LORD will be your rear guard.
Then you will call, and the LORD will answer;
    you will cry for help, and he will say: Here am I.

—ISAIAH 58:3; 6–9

A recent news feature chronicled the growing search for stress relief through spas, massage, pills, and exercise tapes. The craving to ease tension has spawned an entire industry, including walk-in backrub stores in shopping malls across the country. The report ended by saying, "Although people will pay to fix their stress, they are not about to change the lifestyle that is causing it."

No matter what the problem, our initial response is to treat the symptoms rather than the cause.

During the days of Isaiah, God's people were not experiencing the Lord's blessing. They went through the motions of worship and couldn't understand why God wasn't noticing their religious efforts (Isaiah 58:3). But while they were fasting, they were also exploiting their workers and fighting among themselves (vv. 3–4). Isaiah condemned their hypocrisy and told them they needed to change. If they would free the oppressed, share with the hungry, house the homeless, and clothe the naked, God would bless them with healing, answered prayer, guidance, strength, and joy.

Religious activity is no substitute for an obedient heart. With God's help—and a willingness to change—we can eliminate the root problems, not just the symptoms.

—DAVID McCASLAND

Ugly Gremlins

The righteous will flourish like a palm tree,
*   they will grow like a cedar of Lebanon;*
planted in the house of the LORD,
*   they will flourish in the courts of our God.*
They will still bear fruit in old age,
*   they will stay fresh and green,*
proclaiming, "The LORD is upright;
*   he is my Rock, and there is no wickedness in him."*

—PSALM 92:12–15

In her book *Less Stress, More Peace*, Verna Birkey refers to a seventy-two-year-old woman named Jo who worried about growing older. Jo called these fears "ugly gremlins." To gain victory over them, she wrote a Declaration of Commitment and Faith, which I quote in part:

"My dear heavenly Father, how can I ever express how grateful I am for Your great care over me through the years? You have been so good. Why then, Lord, do these ugly gremlins come into my thinking? I worry about losing this wonderful husband that You have given me. Will I have to suffer a long illness before You take me home? What if I end up in a rest home? What if I become senile?

"There now, I've verbalized them! Those ugly gremlins! Lord, I now commit all these worries about old age to You. I will claim the promise You have given me in Psalm 92, that I shall still bring forth fruit in my old age. Each time one of these fears comes up, I will go back and review this commitment until I have peace. I can trust You with my old age. I praise You, Lord!"

Why not write your own Declaration of Commitment and Faith concerning your "ugly gremlins"?　　—JOANIE YODER

Strengthened for the Work

Then Haggai, the LORD's messenger, gave this message of the LORD to the people: "I am with you," declares the LORD. So the LORD stirred up the spirit of Zerubbabel son of Shealtiel, governor of Judah, and the spirit of Joshua son of Jehozadak, the high priest, and the spirit of the whole remnant of the people. They came and began to work on the house of the LORD Almighty, their God, on the twenty-fourth day of the sixth month in the second year of King Darius.

On the twenty-first day of the seventh month, the word of the LORD came through the prophet Haggai: "Speak to Zerubbabel son of Shealtiel, governor of Judah, to Joshua son of Jehozadak, the high priest, and to the remnant of the people. Ask them, 'Who of you is left who saw this house in its former glory? How does it look to you now? Does it not seem to you like nothing? But now be strong, O Zerubbabel,' declares the LORD. 'Be strong, O Joshua son of Jehozadak, the high priest. Be strong, all you people of the land,' declares the LORD, 'and work. For I am with you,' declares the LORD Almighty. 'This is what I covenanted with you when you came out of Egypt. And my Spirit remains among you. Do not fear.'
— HAGGAI 1:13–2:5

It was my privilege to spend time with a group of church leaders at a pastors' conference. It soon became evident that the rugged demands of the pastorate and the idealistic expectations of some congregations were taking a toll on these faithful servants of the Lord. Some were burned out and emotionally exhausted. Others were asking hard questions about the primary responsibilities of a pastor and how to find time for everything.

Some were stressed by the "watchdog" members of their church—you know, the kind who watch every little move and let you know if you're even slightly out of step. Other pastors wondered how to know when it's time to leave.

In one meeting, the conference director brought an encouraging message from the book of Haggai. He reminded these faithful laborers in Christ's church of Haggai's words from the Lord to Zerubbabel, the leader of the project to rebuild the temple: "Be strong" (2:4), "I am with you" (v. 4), "I will bless you" (v. 19), and "I have chosen you" (v. 23).

These words from the Lord should encourage all who are weary in the work of God. If you're stressed and exhausted, remember that God is with you, and He will strengthen you for the work He's called you to do.   —DAVE EGNER

How to Handle Fear

Be merciful to me, O God, for men hotly pursue me;
  all day long they press their attack.
My slanderers pursue me all day long;
  many are attacking me in their pride.
When I am afraid,
  I will trust in you.
In God, whose word I praise,
  in God I trust; I will not be afraid.
  What can mortal man do to me? . . .
Then my enemies will turn back
  when I call for help.
  By this I will know that God is for me.
In God, whose word I praise,
  in the LORD, whose word I praise--
in God I trust; I will not be afraid.
  What can man do to me?
I am under vows to you, O God;
  I will present my thank offerings to you.
For you have delivered me from death
  and my feet from stumbling,
that I may walk before God
  in the light of life.

—PSALM 56:1–4; 9–13

*S*ome years ago as I lay in a hospital bed, I overheard two women talking in a waiting room outside my door. Evidently the husband of one of them was in critical condition. She had been under extreme stress and was greatly concerned about his recovery. She said to her friend, "You know, when you're as worried as I am, you just have to smoke!"

That made me think about how people handle their fears. Some turn to alcohol, others turn to food, and some to busyness. The psalmist gave us a better solution to the problem of fear. He said, "When I am afraid, I will trust in You" (56:3). It's tragic when we turn to something other than the Lord to fill the void or cover up the pain we're feeling.

If we have put our faith in God's Son, Jesus Christ, we can have confidence that our heavenly Father sees us in our trials and has promised His protection. In times of distress, we can place our trust in the Lord. He wants us to call on Him so that He can encourage us with His presence and give us His peace.

As you rest in the Lord and rely on Him today, you will be able to say with the psalmist, "When I am afraid, I will trust in You."

—RICHARD DE HAAN

Work Opportunity

As God's fellow workers we urge you not to receive God's grace in vain. For he says,

> "In the time of my favor I heard you,
>   and in the day of salvation I helped you."

I tell you, now is the time of God's favor, now is the day of salvation.

We put no stumbling block in anyone's path, so that our ministry will not be discredited. Rather, as servants of God we commend ourselves in every way: in great endurance; in troubles, hardships and distresses; in beatings, imprisonments and riots; in hard work, sleepless nights and hunger; in purity, understanding, patience and kindness; in the Holy Spirit and in sincere love; in truthful speech and in the power of God; with weapons of righteousness in the right hand and in the left; through glory and dishonor, bad report and good report; genuine, yet regarded as impostors; known, yet regarded as unknown; dying, and yet we live on; beaten, and yet not killed; sorrowful, yet always rejoicing; poor, yet making many rich; having nothing, and yet possessing everything.

—2 CORINTHIANS 6:1–10

*I*magine an eighteen-year-old searching the want ads for a summer job. Because he likes the outdoors, his interest is drawn to an ad about a national wildlife and fish refuge. It lists several job openings, but instead of promising attractive benefits and lucrative pay, the ad warns that the work will include "exposure to heat, humidity, rain, mud, millions of biting mosquitoes, poisonous plants, barbed wire, and hard work." The pay is minimum wage.

Now imagine that the eighteen-year-old is a Christian looking for meaningful spiritual service. His eyes rest on 2 Corinthians 6. There he finds the apostle Paul describing the highest calling of all, an opportunity to work for the Lord. But again the job description is very candid about some of the stresses that go with the work. Although Paul's experiences as an apostle were unique, his words remind all readers that serving the Lord is not one big vacation. It requires great care and effort, and it takes the highest commitment.

Yes, the challenge of serving Christ is without parallel and will require sacrifice. But we are not in it alone, and that makes all the difference. No price is too great to pay for the privilege of working for the Lord! — MART DE HAAN

Hurry Sickness

But whatever was to my profit I now consider loss for the sake of Christ. What is more, I consider everything a loss compared to the surpassing greatness of knowing Christ Jesus my Lord, for whose sake I have lost all things. I consider them rubbish, that I may gain Christ and be found in him, not having a righteousness of my own that comes from the law, but that which is through faith in Christ—the righteousness that comes from God and is by faith. I want to know Christ and the power of his resurrection and the fellowship of sharing in his sufferings, becoming like him in his death, and so, somehow, to attain to the resurrection from the dead.

Not that I have already obtained all this, or have already been made perfect, but I press on to take hold of that for which Christ Jesus took hold of me. Brothers, I do not consider myself yet to have taken hold of it. But one thing I do: Forgetting what is behind and straining toward what is ahead, I press on toward the goal to win the prize for which God has called me heavenward in Christ Jesus.

All of us who are mature should take such a view of things. And if on some point you think differently, that too God will make clear to you. Only let us live up to what we have already attained.
—PHILIPPIANS 3:7–16

urry up!" "You're too slow!" "We're late!" How often do impatient words like these crop up in our speech, revealing our fast pace of life? If we're not careful, we become people living in the fast lane, demanding quick arrivals and instant results. Stress experts call this problem "hurry sickness."

In Philippians 3, the apostle Paul's testimony of lifelong growth reminds us that Christian maturity can be encouraged but not hurried. In his book *Overcomers through the Cross,* Paul Billheimer says that just as God takes time to make an oak tree, He takes time to make a saint. Christian growth is a process.

Billheimer writes, "An unripe apple is not fit to eat, but we should not therefore condemn it. It is not yet ready for eating because God is not done making it. It is a phase of its career and good in its place."

Are you feeling impatient over your spiritual growth? Remember, God is not finished with you—nor does He expect to be until He calls you home. Only make sure that your goal is to know Christ and to become more like Him. Then slowly but surely, under blue skies and stormy, He will bring you to maturity. It's His sure cure for "hurry sickness."   —JOANIE YODER

Groans Now, Glory Later

The Spirit himself testifies with our spirit that we are God's children. Now if we are children, then we are heirs—heirs of God and co-heirs with Christ, if indeed we share in his sufferings in order that we may also share in his glory.

I consider that our present sufferings are not worth comparing with the glory that will be revealed in us. The creation waits in eager expectation for the sons of God to be revealed. For the creation was subjected to frustration, not by its own choice, but by the will of the one who subjected it, in hope that the creation itself will be liberated from its bondage to decay and brought into the glorious freedom of the children of God.

—ROMANS 8:16–21

I once heard of a Christian seminar titled "How to Live a Stress-Free Life." Such an unrealistic hope promptly made me stressful! Yet we all long for relief.

A Christian friend of mine whose family is experiencing tough times admits feeling let down by God. She said, "I've prayed, agonized, and claimed promises, but nothing changes. The frustrating thing is that I know He has the power to get us out of this. I've seen Him do it before, but this time He's silent."

Larry Crabb, in his book *Inside Out,* emphasizes that our only hope for complete relief from hardship is to be with Jesus in heaven. "Until then," he says, "we either groan or pretend we don't." He adds, "The experience of groaning, however, is precisely what modern Christianity so often tries to help us escape."

My friend is groaning, and she's not pretending she isn't. Like all of us, she simply wants things to change. But the fact is, something is changing—she is! Paul assured us in 2 Corinthians 4:17 that our present sufferings are lightweight and brief compared with the weighty and eternal changes those sufferings are producing in us. So let's not lose heart. There's glory ahead! (Romans 8:18).   —Joanie Yoder

His Good Purpose

And we know that in all things God works for the good of those who love him, who have been called according to his purpose. For those God foreknew he also predestined to be conformed to the likeness of his Son, that he might be the firstborn among many brothers. And those he predestined, he also called; those he called, he also justified; those he justified, he also glorified.

What, then, shall we say in response to this? If God is for us, who can be against us? He who did not spare his own Son, but gave him up for us all—how will he not also, along with him, graciously give us all things? Who will bring any charge against those whom God has chosen? It is God who justifies. Who is he that condemns? Christ Jesus, who died—more than that, who was raised to life—is at the right hand of God and is also interceding for us. Who shall separate us from the love of Christ? . . .

In all these things we are more than conquerors through him who loved us. For I am convinced that neither death nor life, neither angels nor demons, neither the present nor the future, nor any powers, neither height nor depth, nor anything else in all creation, will be able to separate us from the love of God that is in Christ Jesus our Lord. —ROMANS 8:28–35; 37–39

Romans 8:28—how easily and how often this Bible reference rolls off our tongues! But perhaps we need to grasp more fully what this verse is really saying.

Randy Alcorn, in a book he has co-authored with his wife, Nanci, offers some insights on Romans 8:28. He quotes the New American Standard Bible translation of this verse: "God causes all things to work together for good." Randy points out that it doesn't say each individual thing is good, but that God works them together for good.

Recalling his boyhood days, Randy tells how he often watched his mother bake cakes. One day when she had all the ingredients set out—flour, sugar, baking powder, raw egg, vanilla—he sneaked a taste of each one. Except for the sugar, they all tasted horrible. Then his mother stirred them together and put the batter in the oven. "It didn't make sense to me," he recalls, "that the combination of individually distasteful things produced such a tasty product."

Randy concludes that God likewise "takes all the undesirable stresses in our lives, mixes them together, puts them under the heat of crisis, and produces a perfect result."

Let's look beyond our immediate circumstances and remember that God has an ultimate good purpose. —JOANIE YODER

Singing While We Walk

I lift up my eyes to the hills—
    where does my help come from?
My help comes from the LORD,
    the Maker of heaven and earth.
He will not let your foot slip—
    he who watches over you will not slumber;
indeed, he who watches over Israel
    will neither slumber nor sleep.
The LORD watches over you—
    the LORD is your shade at your right hand;
the sun will not harm you by day,
    nor the moon by night.
The LORD will keep you from all harm—
    he will watch over your life;
the LORD will watch over your coming and going
    both now and forevermore.

—PSALM 121

*S*inging makes our journey through life easier. Singing takes a lot of stress out of the trip and smooths over many of the rough places in the road, especially when we sing praises to the God who made heaven and earth and who cares for us each mile of the way.

The Hebrew pilgrims sang Psalm 121 as they walked to Jerusalem to celebrate the yearly feast. The song not only passed the time, but it reminded them of the ways God took care of them. The Hebrew word for *keep* is repeated six times in the psalm (though in some versions it is translated "preserve," "protect," or "guard"). This song uses four word pictures to help God's people see Him as the One who keeps them secure on their journey through life.

1. He is the God of the towering hills, who gives help to His people (vv. 1–2).
2. He is the God of the night watch, who neither slumbers nor sleeps (vv. 3–4).
3. He is the God who provides friendly shade to protect from the elements that might hurt us (vv. 5–6).
4. He is the God of the house and of the road, who looks after us in all our comings and goings (vv. 7–8).

Keep trusting God. He keeps you in His keeping.

—Haddon Robinson

When to Believe

[Moses answered], "The LORD will fight for you; you need only to be still."

Then the LORD said to Moses, "Why are you crying out to me? Tell the Israelites to move on. Raise your staff and stretch out your hand over the sea to divide the water so that the Israelites can go through the sea on dry ground. I will harden the hearts of the Egyptians so that they will go in after them. And I will gain glory through Pharaoh and all his army, through his chariots and his horsemen. The Egyptians will know that I am the LORD when I gain glory through Pharaoh, his chariots and his horsemen.". . .

Then Moses stretched out his hand over the sea, and all that night the LORD drove the sea back with a strong east wind and turned it into dry land. The waters were divided, and the Israelites went through the sea on dry ground, with a wall of water on their right and on their left . . .

And when the Israelites saw the great power the LORD displayed against the Egyptians, the people feared the LORD and put their trust in him and in Moses his servant.

—EXODUS 14:14–18; 21–22; 31

After God freed the people of Israel from their Egyptian captors, Moses reminded them that God had sworn to give them "the land of the Canaanites" (Exodus 13:11). That promise should have given them hope even in the most stressful times as they journeyed through the desert. Yet when they felt trapped between the Red Sea and the Egyptians, their faith failed.

Turning to Moses, they said, "It would have been better for us to serve the Egyptians than to die in the wilderness" (Exodus 14:12). Although the situation looked bad, this was when they should have believed that God was going to rescue them. Despite their lack of faith, God divided the waters and saved them from the advancing army. Only then did the people fear and believe God (Exodus 14:31).

We too have promises from God. He said, "Never will I leave you; never will I forsake you" (Hebrews 13:5), yet we sometimes face our trials as if God has abandoned us. He told us, "If we ask anything according to his will, he hears us" (1 John 5:14), yet we often tackle life's problems without first committing them to God.

During our times of difficulty, we need to rely on God's promises. That's how faith grows strong!   —DAVE BRANON

Remain Faithful

Dear friends, do not be surprised at the painful trial you are suffering, as though something strange were happening to you. But rejoice that you participate in the sufferings of Christ, so that you may be overjoyed when his glory is revealed. If you are insulted because of the name of Christ, you are blessed, for the Spirit of glory and of God rests on you. If you suffer, it should not be as a murderer or thief or any other kind of criminal, or even as a meddler. However, if you suffer as a Christian, do not be ashamed, but praise God that you bear that name. For it is time for judgment to begin with the family of God; and if it begins with us, what will the outcome be for those who do not obey the gospel of God? And,

> *"If it is hard for the righteous to be saved,
> what will become of the ungodly and the sinner?"*

So then, those who suffer according to God's will should commit themselves to their faithful Creator and continue to do good. —1 PETER 4:12–19

---

*D*uring the uprisings in Zaire in 1964, the rebels were treating all outsiders with suspicion. Americans and Belgians were particularly despised because their nations were backing the government in power. The day came when the rebel forces rounded up many foreigners, including Al Larson, his wife, and their fellow missionaries.

Al was thrown into a little building with nine other men. Only three were believers, and they made an important decision: They were in Zaire to proclaim Christ and serve Him, and they would continue to do that.

The days that followed were far from pleasant. They lived in constant fear. On two occasions the men were loaded into vehicles and told they were going to be executed.

The Christians continued to witness and serve. Finally they were dramatically rescued. When those ten men left that little shack for the last time, all of them were believers in Jesus Christ!

Times getting rough? Being persecuted? Under extreme stress? Scared? Make the same decision those believers did, and continue to serve Christ. Even if you are discouraged and feel like quitting, decide that throughout the ordeal you are going to remain faithful. —DAVE EGNER

The Need for Stress

Arise, LORD! Lift up your hand, O God.
Do not forget the helpless.
Why does the wicked man revile God?
Why does he say to himself,
"He won't call me to account"?
But you, O God, do see trouble and grief;
you consider it to take it in hand.
The victim commits himself to you;
you are the helper of the fatherless.
Break the arm of the wicked and evil man;
call him to account for his wickedness
that would not be found out.
The Lord is King for ever and ever;
the nations will perish from his land.
You hear, O Lord, the desire of the afflicted;
you encourage them, and you listen to their cry,
defending the fatherless and the oppressed,
in order that man, who is of the earth, may terrify
no more.

—PSALM 10:12–18

When crime in the streets of Detroit reached alarming levels, a prominent community leader called for the revival of STRESS to fight the problem. The STRESS in view, however, had more to it than merely elevating someone's blood pressure. STRESS is an acronym that stands for Stop The Robberies and Enjoy Safe Streets. It was a discontinued program that had employed undercover policemen who served as street decoys to bait and then nab criminals. The theory was that when criminals learned that disguised officers were roaming the streets, they would think twice before hitting a vulnerable person.

Psalm 10 reminds us that criminals, by nature, do not experience enough of the right kind of stress. The criminal mind doesn't fear the Lord. But such a person, whether thief, gossip, or liar, is deceiving himself. The Lord is always there. He is there with all of the authority of heaven, hell, and eternity at His command. He is there unseen, undercover.

Lord, help us today to sense that You are near. Help us to experience the right kind of stress — not a cowering fear but a deep reverence for You and Your truth. We want to be sensitive to wrong so that we will always want to do right. We have no fear of losing Your love but of quenching and grieving Your Spirit.   —MART DE HAAN

A New God

We always thank God for all of you, mentioning you in our prayers. We continually remember before our God and Father your work produced by faith, your labor prompted by love, and your endurance inspired by hope in our Lord Jesus Christ.

For we know, brothers loved by God, that he has chosen you, because our gospel came to you not simply with words, but also with power, with the Holy Spirit and with deep conviction. You know how we lived among you for your sake. You became imitators of us and of the Lord; in spite of severe suffering, you welcomed the message with the joy given by the Holy Spirit. And so you became a model to all the believers in Macedonia and Achaia. The Lord's message rang out from you not only in Macedonia and Achaia—your faith in God has become known everywhere. Therefore we do not need to say anything about it, for they themselves report what kind of reception you gave us. They tell how you turned to God from idols to serve the living and true God, and to wait for his Son from heaven, whom he raised from the dead—Jesus, who rescues us from the coming wrath.

—1 THESSALONIANS 1:2–10

Tim Burke is a faithful Christian, loyal husband, and good father, but he wasn't always that way. Who is Tim Burke? He's a former All-Star relief pitcher for the Montreal Expos. Here's what he said about the way he used to be: "Baseball was my life. When I became a pro ballplayer, baseball went from just being a game to a god."

If Tim didn't perform up to expectations, his team might send him home. Pressure to perform mounted. To handle the growing stress, he turned to alcohol. Soon he lost his ability to pitch effectively. Then his young marriage developed serious problems. When things were at their worst, Tim and his wife Christine were invited to a Bible study. For the first time he realized that Christianity is not merely trying to be a good person, it's a relationship with Christ.

After a few weeks of struggling, Tim asked Jesus to forgive him, and he gave his life to Christ. Three changes occurred: Tim saw his wife with truly loving eyes, he lost his desire to drink, and he stopped making baseball his god. Life became worthwhile.

Have you been worshiping something in the place of Christ? It may not be a professional sport, but it could be your job, your home, or wealth. If so, you need a new God. Turn to Jesus. He is the true God. —DAVE EGNER

A Tested String

Shout with joy to God, all the earth!
   Sing the glory of his name;
   make his praise glorious!
Say to God, "How awesome are your deeds!
   So great is your power
   that your enemies cringe before you.
All the earth bows down to you;
   they sing praise to you,
   they sing praise to your name."   Selah
Come and see what God has done,
   how awesome his works in man's behalf!
He turned the sea into dry land,
   they passed through the waters on foot—
   come, let us rejoice in him.
He rules forever by his power,
   his eyes watch the nations—
   let not the rebellious rise up against him.   Selah
Praise our God, O peoples,
   let the sound of his praise be heard;
he has preserved our lives
   and kept our feet from slipping.
For you, O God, tested us;
   you refined us like silver.   —PSALM 66:1–10

A talented violinist was scheduled to play before a very critical audience. Although she had a fine instrument, she was not satisfied with the quality of its sound. So she said to her father, "This violin must yield its full resonance and vibration of tone. I'm going out to buy some tested strings."

When asked what tested strings were, she replied, "First they're put on a rack and stretched and strained to take all the vacillation out of them. Then they are hammered and put through an acid test. This is what enables them to produce a perfect and full tone." When she attached the tested strings and tuned the instrument, the music was noticeably more warm and rich than before.

If our lives are going to produce beautiful music for the Lord, testing is imperative. We all tend to vacillate. Sometimes we are up; sometimes we are down. Sometimes we are hot; sometimes we are cold. This hinders the spiritual tone God desires. Although we don't enjoy the stretch, the strain, and the stress, what God-honoring results they can produce!

Just as a tested string gives the highest quality of sound, so Christians who accept their trials and learn to profit from them are able to bring the greatest glory to the Master Musician.

—Paul Van Gorder

How to Manage Stress

Do not fret because of evil men
  or be envious of those who do wrong;
for like the grass they will soon wither,
  like green plants they will soon die away.
Trust in the LORD and do good;
dwell in the land and enjoy safe pasture.
Delight yourself in the LORD
  and he will give you the desires of your heart.
Commit your way to the LORD;
  trust in him and he will do this:
He will make your righteousness shine like the dawn,
  the justice of your cause like the noonday sun.
Be still before the LORD and wait patiently for him;
    do not fret when men succeed in their ways,
    when they carry out their wicked schemes.
Refrain from anger and turn from wrath;
    do not fret—it leads only to evil.   —PSALM 37:1–8

*L*aurie Jones, writing in *The Baltimore Sun,* emphasizes that it is not necessary to be victimized by stress. She points out that "you, not outside events, control how extensively stress affects your life."

Jones quotes stress-management consultant Donald Tubesing, who says that stress is our response to the situation, not the situation itself. He gives this example: "If you get stuck in traffic, you can work yourself up . . . and yell at anyone who beeps his horn. Or you could view the time you're sitting there as the only uninterrupted 15 minutes you'll have all day."

John Curtis, founder and director of the University of Wisconsin Stress Management Institute, says, "I believe 90 percent of stress is brought on by not living in the present moment—worrying about what's already happened, what's going to happen, or what could happen."

The advice of these stress management experts can be helpful. Our best counsel, however, comes from Psalm 37. When faced with trouble, we should "Be still before the LORD and wait patiently for Him" (v. 7). As we ask for God's help, claim His promises, and trust Him to carry us through, we can relax and stop worrying.

That's how to manage stress.   —RICHARD DE HAAN

Renewed Hope

This is the word that came to Jeremiah from the LORD *:"Go down to the potter's house, and there I will give you my message." So I went down to the potter's house, and I saw him working at the wheel. But the pot he was shaping from the clay was marred in his hands; so the potter formed it into another pot, shaping it as seemed best to him.*

Then the word of the LORD *came to me: "O house of Israel, can I not do with you as this potter does?" declares the* LORD. *"Like clay in the hand of the potter, so are you in my hand, O house of Israel. If at any time I announce that a nation or kingdom is to be uprooted, torn down and destroyed, and if that nation I warned repents of its evil, then I will relent and not inflict on it the disaster I had planned. And if at another time I announce that a nation or kingdom is to be built up and planted, and if it does evil in my sight and does not obey me, then I will reconsider the good I had intended to do for it.*

"Now therefore say to the people of Judah and those living in Jerusalem, 'This is what the LORD *says: Look! I am preparing a disaster for you and devising a plan against you. So turn from your evil ways, each one of you, and reform your ways and your actions.'"*

—JEREMIAH 18:1–11

*W*riting in *The Reaper,* Joanie Yoder told of reaching a point of despair in her role as a pastor's wife. She cited some of the stresses she faced: sharing her husband twenty-four hours a day, resenting perfectionist standards, feeling guilty about recurring bitterness and anger, and having no one to share her feelings with. Gradually she became so discouraged that she was ready to give up.

Mrs. Yoder tells what happened next. "One day I opened my sorely neglected Bible to the writings of the prophet Jeremiah . . . As I read, I watched over Jeremiah's shoulder as the potter worked a lump of clay on his wheel. I began to get emotionally involved when the clay became marred in the potter's hand. Between the lines I assumed the potter would toss aside the lump of spoiled clay to take up another, hoping for better results. For a moment my life was that lump of clay, and I felt the old nagging fear that God, like this potter, might lay aside my disappointing life and take up another to do His work. But . . . I read on to see what the potter really did with the clay: 'and he formed it into another pot, shaping it as seemed best to him!' As if written for me alone, the next verse read, 'Can I not do with you as this potter does? declares the Lord. Like clay in the hand of the potter, so are you in My hand.' "

With renewed hope, Mrs. Yoder realized that God was molding her for His use. What confidence this can give us as we face life's trials!
—DAVE EGNER

Patiently Waiting on God

The LORD is *my light and my salvation;*
Whom shall I fear?
The Lord is the strength of my life;
Of whom shall I be afraid?
When the wicked came against me
To eat up my flesh,
My enemies and foes,
They stumbled and fell.
Though an army may encamp against me,
My heart shall not fear;
Though war may rise against me,
In this I will be confident . . .
I would have lost heart, unless I had believed
That I would see the goodness of the LORD
In the land of the living.
Wait on the LORD;
Be of good courage,
And He shall strengthen your heart;
Wait, I say, on the LORD!

—PSALM 27:1–3; 13–14 (NKJV)

We are all in such a hurry! Yet the best things that God has for us often take time to mature. That's why we must patiently wait on Him and not run before Him. Someone has said, "Give God time, and even when the knife flashes in the air, the ram will be seen in the thicket. Give God time, and even when Pharaoh's host is on Israel's heels, a path through the waters will be suddenly opened. Give God time, and when the bed of the brook is dry, Elijah shall hear the Guiding Voice."

Hebrews 12:1 tells us to "run with endurance" the race set before us. George Matheson wrote, "We commonly associate patience with lying down. We think of it as the angel that guards the couch of the invalid. Yet there is a patience that I believe to be harder—the patience that can run. To lie down in the time of grief, to be quiet under the stroke of adverse fortune, implies a great strength; but I know of something that implies a strength greater still: it is the power to work under stress; to have a great weight at your heart and still run; to have a deep anguish in your spirit and still perform the daily tasks. It is a Christlike thing! The hardest thing is that most of us are called to exercise our patience, not in the sickbed but in the street." To wait is hard, to do it with "good courage" is harder!

Do not try to hasten the unfolding of God's bud of promise; you will only spoil the perfect flower. "By your patience possess your souls" (Luke 21:19 NKJV).   —HENRY BOSCH

But I Need Patience!

Consider it pure joy, my brothers, whenever you face trials of many kinds, because you know that the testing of your faith develops perseverance. Perseverance must finish its work so that you may be mature and complete, not lacking anything. If any of you lacks wisdom, he should ask God, who gives generously to all without finding fault, and it will be given to him. But when he asks, he must believe and not doubt, because he who doubts is like a wave of the sea, blown and tossed by the wind. That man should not think he will receive anything from the Lord; he is a double-minded man, unstable in all he does.

The brother in humble circumstances ought to take pride in his high position. But the one who is rich should take pride in his low position, because he will pass away like a wild flower. For the sun rises with scorching heat and withers the plant; its blossom falls and its beauty is destroyed. In the same way, the rich man will fade away even while he goes about his business.

Blessed is the man who perseveres under trial, because when he has stood the test, he will receive the crown of life that God has promised to those who love him. —JAMES 1:2–12

*I*f you never lose patience waiting in a checkout line, living with your husband or wife or children or roommate, or just going about your daily duties, then read no further. This article is not for you. But if you are normal, you'll welcome the opportunity to learn how to gain some patience. Here's the formula: *Pressure Produces Patience*. That's the thrust of Romans 5:3, for the word *tribulation* means pressure or affliction. And the word *perseverance* means patience or endurance.

The story is told of a woman who had little patience. So she went to her minister and said, "Pastor, pray that God will give me patience!"

"Let's bow our heads right now and bring your need to the Lord," the pastor responded. He began, "Heavenly Father, send trials and difficulties into the life of this, Your child. May she have much tribulation."

Before he could say another word, the woman interrupted, "But Pastor, I need patience, not tribulation!"

"I know," came the gentle reply, "but God says this is the best way to learn it."

James told us to "consider it pure joy" when we fall into various trials because the testing of our faith produces patience (James 1:2, 3). The moral fiber of perseverance can grow when nourished by stress. So the next time you feel the pressures of trying to live as a Christian in a hostile world, pray for strength and say to the Lord, "Thank You for another opportunity to learn patience!"   —DENNIS DE HAAN

I Dreaded Going Back

"Ah, Sovereign LORD, you have made the heavens and the earth by your great power and outstretched arm. Nothing is too hard for you. You show love to thousands but bring the punishment for the fathers' sins into the laps of their children after them. O great and powerful God, whose name is the LORD Almighty, great are your purposes and mighty are your deeds. Your eyes are open to all the ways of men; you reward everyone according to his conduct and as his deeds deserve. You performed miraculous signs and wonders in Egypt and have continued them to this day, both in Israel and among all mankind, and have gained the renown that is still yours. You brought your people Israel out of Egypt with signs and wonders, by a mighty hand and an outstretched arm and with great terror. You gave them this land you had sworn to give their forefathers, a land flowing with milk and honey.

—JEREMIAH 32:17–22

*I*t was in a Sunday morning service that missionary Lois Walsh was bidding farewell to the church. Within three hours the plane would be in the air, carrying her, her husband, and their three young children on the first leg of their journey back to Brazil. The weeks preceding had been hectic, filled with hard work and difficult obstacles. Now Lois stood before us, looking fresh and unruffled. I wondered what she was going to say.

First she thanked the church people for their friendship and help during their furlough. Then she admitted honestly, "I dreaded going back." It was not the missionary work, she explained, but all the effort of moving her children. Furthermore, a month after arriving on the field, they would have to move again. She had wondered how she could do it. Then she called our attention to Jeremiah 32:17. "One day," she said, "I was particularly dreading all the hard work and emotional stress of the return. I felt weak and inadequate. In my Bible reading for that day, however, I came to Jeremiah 32. I thought about the power of our Creator God. And I came to the words that speak of Him, 'Nothing is too hard for You.' I realized anew that I wouldn't have to do it all alone—that all the strength of God was at my disposal. He is my Helper."

Are you facing some difficult problems? Are you overwhelmed with work? Is the emotional strain getting to you? Remember, nothing is too hard for God!   —DAVE EGNER

God is our refuge and strength,
    an ever-present help in trouble.
Therefore we will not fear, though the earth give way
    and the mountains fall into the heart of the sea,
though its waters roar and foam
    and the mountains quake with their surging.   Selah
There is a river whose streams make glad the city of God,
    the holy place where the Most High dwells.
God is within her, she will not fall;
    God will help her at break of day.
Nations are in uproar, kingdoms fall;
    he lifts his voice, the earth melts.
The Lord Almighty is with us;
    the God of Jacob is our fortress.   Selah
Come and see the works of the Lord,
    the desolations he has brought on the earth.
He makes wars cease to the ends of the earth;
    he breaks the bow and shatters the spear,
    he burns the shields with fire.
"Be still, and know that I am God;
    I will be exalted among the nations,
    I will be exalted in the earth."
The Lord Almighty is with us;
    the God of Jacob is our fortress.   Selah
                                        —Psalm 46

*S*tudies have been made on how much stress we experience in adjusting to change. Researchers rated more than forty situations, giving to them "life-change units." To name a few, the death of a spouse rated 100 on the scale of impact; divorce, 73; fired from a job, 47; death of a close friend, 37; son or daughter leaving home, 29; begin or end school, 26; change in residence, 20; and vacation, 13. An accumulation of 200 life-change units in a single year, say the experts, is usually followed by some type of emotional or psychiatric disorder.

It would seem that to keep our lives on a steady course, we must never allow the stress level to exceed the 200 mark. While we must always be sensible in the way we order our lives, we can't engage in a continual quest for stress-free living. Many pressure-producing circumstances are beyond our control, the result of progress—yes, a normal part of living in this twenty-first-century world. Stress is woven into the fabric of our existence.

The writer of Psalm 46 discovered a way to face unsettling, earth-shaking changes, such as mountains falling "into the heart of the sea," nations raging, and kingdoms being moved. He found refuge in God, and he discovered quietness of heart in the knowledge that the Lord is in control (v. 10). For him the only way to counteract the effects of mounting life-change units was to abandon himself to the unchanging One who is a "very present help in trouble." I can think of no better solution, can you?
—Dennis De Haan

Carrying Care

"Therefore I tell you, do not worry about your life, what you will eat or drink; or about your body, what you will wear. Is not life more important than food, and the body more important than clothes? Look at the birds of the air; they do not sow or reap or store away in barns, and yet your heavenly Father feeds them. Are you not much more valuable than they? Who of you by worrying can add a single hour to his life?

"And why do you worry about clothes? See how the lilies of the field grow. They do not labor or spin. Yet I tell you that not even Solomon in all his splendor was dressed like one of these. If that is how God clothes the grass of the field, which is here today and tomorrow is thrown into the fire, will he not much more clothe you, O you of little faith? So do not worry, saying, 'What shall we eat?' or 'What shall we drink?' or 'What shall we wear?' For the pagans run after all these things, and your heavenly Father knows that you need them. But seek first his kingdom and his righteousness, and all these things will be given to you as well. Therefore do not worry about tomorrow, for tomorrow will worry about itself. Each day has enough trouble of its own."

—MATTHEW 6:25–34

*N*o one ever said life would be easy. After all, we live in a fallen world, and we are subject to all the heartaches and disappointments that accompany a normal existence. Anxiety, worry, and care go along with living; it's what we do with them that really counts. This is where Christians have the advantage. They have a Savior who bears their burdens.

How shallow is the world's way of handling anxiety! Every year a group of famous men, all members of an exclusive club in California, get together for an elaborate lakeside ritual called "The Cremation of Care." *The Wall Street Journal* reported one man as saying that the ceremony is intended to symbolize "that whatever our problems, our pressures, our anxieties in the real world, this is a special time, a time to go away and invite a different range of emotions and feelings." An effigy of "Care" is burned, and a band plays "Hot Time in the Old Town Tonight." Every effort is made to escape all feelings of anxiety. But after the weekend is over, the worries always return. The same old stress pattern is in effect again because the underlying problems are still there.

Believers in Christ don't have to stage elaborate rituals to escape their worries for a brief time so they can face reality again. They can go to the Savior in prayer, who will lift their cares and quiet their troubled hearts

Are you still trying to shoulder life's burdens by yourself? Then cast them all upon Christ, who "cares for you" (1 Peter 5:7).

—DAVE EGNER

Let's Take a Break

When Jesus had called the Twelve together, he gave them power and authority to drive out all demons and to cure diseases, and he sent them out to preach the kingdom of God and to heal the sick. He told them: "Take nothing for the journey—no staff, no bag, no bread, no money, no extra tunic. Whatever house you enter, stay there until you leave that town. If people do not welcome you, shake the dust off your feet when you leave their town, as a testimony against them." So they set out and went from village to village, preaching the gospel and healing people everywhere.

Now Herod the tetrarch heard about all that was going on. And he was perplexed, because some were saying that John had been raised from the dead, others that Elijah had appeared, and still others that one of the prophets of long ago had come back to life. But Herod said, "I beheaded John. Who, then, is this I hear such things about?" And he tried to see him.

When the apostles returned, they reported to Jesus what they had done. Then he took them with him and they withdrew by themselves to a town called Bethsaida . . .   —LUKE 9:1–10

According to tradition, when the apostle John was overseer in Ephesus, his hobby was raising pigeons. It is said that on one occasion another elder passed his house as he returned from hunting and saw John playing with one of his birds. The man gently chided him for spending his time so frivolously.

John looked at the hunter's bow and remarked that the string was loose. "Yes," said the elder, "I always loosen the string of my bow when it's not in use. If it stayed tight, it would lose its resilience and fail me in the hunt."

John responded, "And I am now relaxing the bow of my mind so that I may be better able to shoot the arrows of divine truth."

We cannot do our best work with nerves taut or frayed from constant pressure. When Jesus' disciples returned from a strenuous preaching mission, their Master recognized their need for rest and invited them to come with Him to a quiet place where they could be refreshed (Mark 6:31).

Hobbies, vacations, and wholesome recreation are vital to a well-balanced, godly life. We lose our effectiveness by keeping our lives so tightly strung that we are always tense. If it seems we can't relax, Jesus may be inviting us to take a break—to "come with me by yourselves to a quiet place and get some rest." —DENNIS DE HAAN

Bring Out the Shine

"But if I go to the east, he is not there;
    if I go to the west, I do not find him.
When he is at work in the north, I do not see him;
    when he turns to the south, I catch no glimpse of him.
But he knows the way that I take;
    when he has tested me, I will come forth as gold.
My feet have closely followed his steps;
    I have kept to his way without turning aside.
I have not departed from the commands of his lips;
    I have treasured the words of his mouth more than my
        daily bread.
But he stands alone, and who can oppose him?
    He does whatever he pleases.
He carries out his decree against me,
    and many such plans he still has in store.
That is why I am terrified before him;
    when I think of all this, I fear him.
God has made my heart faint;
    the Almighty has terrified me.
Yet I am not silenced by the darkness,
    by the thick darkness that covers my face."

—JOB 23:8–17

Many years ago I bought a 1964 Volkswagen from my neighbor. The car was mechanically sound, but the outside looked pretty rough. Dents marred its surface, and dirt and grime had dulled its once deep blue color.

As time passed, I wondered if its original luster and beauty could be restored. I was sure its bumps could be eliminated, but what about the finish? So I began to experiment on some of the worst spots. Much to my delight, I discovered that with a lot of elbow grease and some rubbing compound my drab little Volkswagen could be brought to a beautiful shine.

We as Christians have the wonderful potential of reflecting the beauty of our Savior. But sin has left its mark on our personalities, and a lot of "road film" needs to be removed before the lovely character of Jesus can be seen in us.

God often brings about this change through the buffing of hardship and trials, for pressure has a way of loosening the dirt and grime of rebellion and selfishness. The Bible tells us that tribulation produces perseverance, character, hope, and confidence by the Holy Spirit (Romans 5:3–5).

We might wish that a speedy "car wash" could do the job, but there's no substitute for the difficulties that can bring out the shine of Christlike character. —DENNIS DE HAAN

Wholesome Humor

Be imitators of God, therefore, as dearly loved children and live a life of love, just as Christ loved us and gave himself up for us as a fragrant offering and sacrifice to God.

But among you there must not be even a hint of sexual immorality, or of any kind of impurity, or of greed, because these are improper for God's holy people. Nor should there be obscenity, foolish talk or coarse joking, which are out of place, but rather thanksgiving. For of this you can be sure: No immoral, impure or greedy person—such a man is an idolater—has any inheritance in the kingdom of Christ and of God. Let no one deceive you with empty words, for because of such things God's wrath comes on those who are disobedient. Therefore do not be partners with them.

For you were once darkness, but now you are light in the Lord. Live as children of light (for the fruit of the light consists in all goodness, righteousness and truth) and find out what pleases the Lord.

—EPHESIANS 5:1–10

Abraham Lincoln faced enormous pressures as president during the Civil War. It was probably his healthy sense of humor that enabled him to bear the strain. When emotions ran high in cabinet meetings, he often told a funny story to break the tension. Laughing at himself kept him from becoming defensive. And a good story with a strong point sometimes won over an opponent.

The spontaneity of humor reflects the way God created man. It is both physically and emotionally beneficial. Laughter can keep a tense situation from ending in bitter words or hard feelings.

Although Jesus was a "man of sorrows, and familiar with suffering" (Isaiah 53:3), I believe He laughed often. Sometimes Jesus used humor to make a point. Imagine a camel trying to squeeze through the eye of a needle! (Matthew 19:24).

But there's also a dark side to humor. Paul called it "coarse joking" and said that it should have no place in the believer's life (Ephesians 5:4). It demeans, degrades, and defiles those who use it and those who hear it.

So what do we laugh at? What kinds of stories do we tell each other? Would Jesus laugh with us? I believe He would—if it were wholesome humor. —DENNIS DE HAAN

Inner Strength

For this reason I kneel before the Father, from whom his whole family in heaven and on earth derives its name. I pray that out of his glorious riches he may strengthen you with power through his Spirit in your inner being, so that Christ may dwell in your hearts through faith. And I pray that you, being rooted and established in love, may have power, together with all the saints, to grasp how wide and long and high and deep is the love of Christ, and to know this love that surpasses knowledge—that you may be filled to the measure of all the fullness of God.

Now to him who is able to do immeasurably more than all we ask or imagine, according to his power that is at work within us, to him be glory in the church and in Christ Jesus throughout all generations, for ever and ever! Amen.

—EPHESIANS 3:14–21

A large company uses suction to extract contaminating substances from steel drums. Powerful pumps draw the materials out of the barrels, but the workers must carefully regulate the force of these pumps. If they take out too much air, the drums will collapse like paper cups because the outer pressure will exceed the inner pressure.

Likewise, when adversity and hardship come into our lives, God must empower us from within, or we will be unable to withstand the pressures from without. True, we get solid support from loved ones and Christian friends, but it is our spiritual inner man, "[strengthened] with power through his Spirit" (Ephesians 3:16), that sustains us and keeps us from crumpling.

The Holy Spirit works to strengthen us and renew our minds as we read the Bible and pray. If we neglect the Scriptures, seldom talk with the Lord, and stop fellowshiping with other believers, we'll grow weak and vulnerable. Then we will be unable to withstand the pressures of temptation or trouble.

If we ask the Lord to develop our inner strength, when life's blows and burdens press upon us we will not cave in.

—DAVE EGNER

Good Medicine

A friend loves at all times,
    and a brother is born for adversity.
A man lacking in judgment strikes hands in pledge
    and puts up security for his neighbor.
He who loves a quarrel loves sin;
    he who builds a high gate invites destruction.
A man of perverse heart does not prosper;
    he whose tongue is deceitful falls into trouble.
To have a fool for a son brings grief;
    there is no joy for the father of a fool.
A cheerful heart is good medicine,
    but a crushed spirit dries up the bones.

—PROVERBS 17:17–22

In a *Better Homes and Gardens* article titled "Laugh Your Way to Good Health," Nick Gallo made an observation that echoes what Solomon wrote thousands of years ago: "A cheerful heart is good medicine, but a crushed spirit dries up the bones" (Proverbs 17:22). Gallo said, "Humor is good medicine—and can actually help keep you in good health." He quoted William F. Fry, MD, who describes laughter as "inner jogging" and says that it's good for a person's cardiovascular system.

Comparing laughter to exercise, Gallo pointed out that when a person laughs heartily, several physical benefits occur. There's a temporary lowering of blood pressure, a decreased rate of breathing, and a reduction in muscle tension. He said that many people sense a "relaxed afterglow." He concluded, "An enduring sense of humor, especially combined with other inner resources such as faith and optimism, appears to be a potent force for better health."

Christians, above all others, should benefit from laughter, because we have the greatest reason to be joyful. Our faith is firmly rooted in God, and our optimism is based on the assurance that our lives are under His wise control.

Don't be afraid to enjoy a good laugh—it's good medicine.

—RICHARD DE HAAN

Weed Control

Then Jesus said to them, "Don't you understand this parable? How then will you understand any parable? The farmer sows the word. Some people are like seed along the path, where the word is sown. As soon as they hear it, Satan comes and takes away the word that was sown in them. Others, like seed sown on rocky places, hear the word and at once receive it with joy. But since they have no root, they last only a short time. When trouble or persecution comes because of the word, they quickly fall away. Still others, like seed sown among thorns, hear the word; but the worries of this life, the deceitfulness of wealth and the desires for other things come in and choke the word, making it unfruitful. Others, like seed sown on good soil, hear the word, accept it, and produce a crop—thirty, sixty or even a hundred times what was sown."

—MARK 4:13–20

The Parrotfeather is an attractive aquatic plant that looks like a forest of small fir trees growing on top of the water. In the springtime it produces a blanket of small, white flowers. But it's a noxious weed. It forms a dense mat of vegetation that covers the surface of lakes and ponds, crowding out native plants and destroying fish and wildlife habitat.

Recently I was hiking by a small lake in Washington State that was choked with Parrotfeather plants. It occurred to me that, like that weed, "the worries of this life, the deceitfulness of wealth and the desires for other things come in and choke the word, making it unfruitful," as Jesus taught in Mark 4:19.

Jesus was talking about how unbelievers receive the gospel, but His words can apply to us as well. Sometimes when we read God's Word, our minds are taken up with troubles, worries, and fears. The pressure of things to be done today and concerns about tomorrow's decisions are "weeds" that can choke the Word and make it unprofitable.

To control the weeds, we must ask God to quiet our hearts so we can pay attention to Him (Psalm 46:10). When we turn our worries over to God, we'll be free to enjoy His presence and hear what He has to say. —DAVID ROPER

Maintaining Character

Therefore, I urge you, brothers, in view of God's mercy, to offer your bodies as living sacrifices, holy and pleasing to God—this is your spiritual act of worship. Do not conform any longer to the pattern of this world, but be transformed by the renewing of your mind. Then you will be able to test and approve what God's will is—his good, pleasing and perfect will.

For by the grace given me I say to every one of you: Do not think of yourself more highly than you ought, but rather think of yourself with sober judgment, in accordance with the measure of faith God has given you. Just as each of us has one body with many members, and these members do not all have the same function, so in Christ we who are many form one body, and each member belongs to all the others. We have different gifts, according to the grace given us. If a man's gift is prophesying, let him use it in proportion to his faith. If it is serving, let him serve; if it is teaching, let him teach; if it is encouraging, let him encourage; if it is contributing to the needs of others, let him give generously; if it is leadership, let him govern diligently; if it is showing mercy, let him do it cheerfully. —ROMANS 12:1–8

*N*ews reporting is a tough business that tends to make reporters hard and unfeeling. That's what Barbara Bradley, a correspondent for National Public Radio, tells aspiring journalists. But she also believes it doesn't have to be that way. "I made a strategic decision when I first fell in love with journalism," Bradley says, "that if I found myself beginning to get tough I would leave the business. It's just a career, and why mortgage your character for a career? Maintaining your character counts for something and you can do it; it's just a decision you have to make."

In every high-pressure situation, we can react like most people, or we can choose to be different. J. B. Phillips translates Romans 12:2 this way: "Don't let the world around you squeeze you into its own mold, but let God remold your minds from within, so that you may prove in practice that the plan of God for you is good, meets all His demands, and moves toward the goal of true maturity."

When we feel pressure to conform, character can stand firm on the bedrock of conviction, saying, "This is God's way, and it is best." Maintaining our character begins and continues with a decision. Let's make it today.   —DAVID McCASLAND

Wind and Worship

One day the angels came to present themselves before the LORD, and Satan also came with them. The LORD said to Satan, "Where have you come from?"

Satan answered the LORD, "From roaming through the earth and going back and forth in it."

Then the LORD said to Satan, "Have you considered my servant Job? There is no one on earth like him; he is blameless and upright, a man who fears God and shuns evil."

"Does Job fear God for nothing?" Satan replied. "Have you not put a hedge around him and his household and everything he has? You have blessed the work of his hands, so that his flocks and herds are spread throughout the land. But stretch out your hand and strike everything he has, and he will surely curse you to your face."

The LORD said to Satan, "Very well, then, everything he has is in your hands, but on the man himself do not lay a finger."

Then Satan went out from the presence of the LORD.

—JOB 1:6–12

Job's calamities were enormous. His oxen and donkeys were stolen. Fire consumed his sheep. Raiders took his camels. But that was just the beginning. A great wind destroyed the house where his sons and daughters were feasting, and they all perished. His loss seemed unbearable! But notice Job's response. He humbled himself and worshiped God (Job 1:20).

On April 2, 1977, the sky north of Olivet, Michigan, grew black and ominous. *Just another severe thunderstorm,* thought Norm Heddon. But when pressure began building in his ears, he instinctively rushed down the basement stairs—which took about five seconds. Then it happened—his house exploded into thousands of pieces from a killer tornado. Minutes later when Norm emerged, he couldn't believe his eyes. All his earthly goods had been swept away, but miraculously his family was unhurt. Bowing in prayer, they thanked God for His goodness. Heddon said, "He has a hand in everything that happens to us."

How can anyone worship while caught up in the fierce winds of adversity? The answer is clear: By anchoring our faith in the love and wisdom of God, we can say through our tears, "The LORD gave and the LORD has taken away; may the name of the LORD be praised" (v. 21).   —DENNIS DE HAAN

The Sandwich Generation

O LORD, you have searched me
  and you know me.
You know when I sit and when I rise;
  you perceive my thoughts from afar.
You discern my going out and my lying down;
  you are familiar with all my ways.
Before a word is on my tongue
  you know it completely, O LORD.
You hem me in—behind and before;
  you have laid your hand upon me.
Such knowledge is too wonderful for me,
  too lofty for me to attain.
Where can I go from your Spirit?
  Where can I flee from your presence?
If I go up to the heavens, you are there;
  if I make my bed in the depths, you are there.
If I rise on the wings of the dawn,
  if I settle on the far side of the sea,
even there your hand will guide me,
  your right hand will hold me fast.
If I say, "Surely the darkness will hide me
  and the light become night around me,"
even the darkness will not be dark to you;
  the night will shine like the day,
  for darkness is as light to you.   —PSALM 139:1–12

The term *sandwich generation* is often used to describe people who are being squeezed between the demands of their children and the responsibility to help their own aging parents. It's not a new dilemma but one that has been complicated by families living far apart, an increasing number of women who work outside their homes, and the pressures faced by single parents.

For the past eight years, my wife's mother has needed full-time care, and our youngest daughter has grown from age seven to fifteen. Two Bible passages have helped us through the ever-changing landscape of being parents and caregivers. The first is 1 Timothy 5:4, "But if a widow has children or grandchildren, these should learn first of all to put their religion into practice by caring for their own family and so repaying their parents and grandparents, for this is pleasing to God. There are many different ways to do this, but the clear command is to care for a parent in need.

The second passage is Psalm 139:5–6. The words of David help us to see that instead of being hemmed in by circumstances, we are surrounded by God's care: "You hem me in—behind and before; you have laid your hand upon me. Such knowledge is too wonderful for me, too lofty for me to attain."

If you're feeling "sandwiched" today, know that the Lord is closer to you than the most pressing circumstances.

—David McCasland

Are You Exhausted?

God saw all that he had made, and it was very good. And there was evening, and there was morning—the sixth day.

Thus the heavens and the earth were completed in all their vast array.

By the seventh day God had finished the work he had been doing; so on the seventh day he rested from all his work.

—GENESIS 1:31–2:2

*I*n today's fast-paced world, many people with day planners, pagers, and cell phones are pushing themselves to the limit. Parents, sometimes with furrowed brows and clenched fists, race from soccer fields to school meetings to piano lessons—grabbing meals on the run and collapsing into bed at night exhausted.

Is it possible that we as followers of Jesus Christ also approach life far too intensely? It seems that we often put ourselves under enormous pressure to succeed and to experience everything we possibly can. When we don't, we can't forgive ourselves for failing to measure up to our own expectations.

But is this the way God wants us to live? When we examine His creation activity in Genesis 1, we see a simple pattern. First was the work of making the universe—everything from atoms to radishes to cats to man. Then came enjoyment—He saw that "it was very good" (v. 31). Then came rest (2:1–2). God rested, not because He was weary but because He was satisfied with the completion of a job well done.

Maybe your hectic schedule and intense lifestyle have robbed you of your sense of humor, peace, joy, and satisfaction in life. If so, follow God's pattern of work, enjoyment, and rest. You'll be amazed at how satisfying life can be. —DAVE EGNER

Choosing Joy

Therefore, since we have been justified through faith, we have peace with God through our Lord Jesus Christ, through whom we have gained access by faith into this grace in which we now stand. And we rejoice in the hope of the glory of God. Not only so, but we also rejoice in our sufferings, because we know that suffering produces perseverance; perseverance, character; and character, hope. And hope does not disappoint us, because God has poured out his love into our hearts by the Holy Spirit, whom he has given us.

You see, at just the right time, when we were still powerless, Christ died for the ungodly. Very rarely will anyone die for a righteous man, though for a good man someone might possibly dare to die. But God demonstrates his own love for us in this: While we were still sinners, Christ died for us.

Since we have now been justified by his blood, how much more shall we be saved from God's wrath through him! For if, when we were God's enemies, we were reconciled to him through the death of his Son, how much more, having been reconciled, shall we be saved through his life! Not only is this so, but we also rejoice in God through our Lord Jesus Christ, through whom we have now received reconciliation. —ROMANS 5:1–11

*M*ost of us don't choose a difficult life—it chooses us. But we can choose our response to it. As someone once said, "Pain is inevitable but misery is optional." Yet when difficulties arise, misery often seems to be the only option.

Author Lloyd Ogilvie tells of a Christian friend who was physically and emotionally depleted because of extreme pressures. A depressed mood engulfed him. When Ogilvie asked him how he was doing, he said grimly, "Well, joy's certainly no option!" Ogilvie replied, "You're right! Joy is no option. It's your responsibility."

Shocked, the friend retorted, "You talk about joy as if it were a duty." Ogilvie responded, "Right again!" He explained that we have a duty to God, ourselves, and others to overcome our moods and to battle through to joy.

In Romans 5, Paul gave these reasons for joy: We have peace with God through Christ, access into grace, and hope of future glory (vv. 1–2). We have assurance that suffering produces perseverance, which in turn builds character and leads to hope (vv. 3–4). We have hope that doesn't disappoint, because God's love has been poured into our hearts (v. 5). —JOANIE YODER

Above Your Problems

Surely the nations are like a drop in a bucket;
   they are regarded as dust on the scales;
   he weighs the islands as though they were fine dust.
Before him all the nations are as nothing;
   they are regarded by him as worthless
   and less than nothing.
To whom, then, will you compare God?
   What image will you compare him to?
As for an idol, a craftsman casts it,
   and a goldsmith overlays it with gold
   and fashions silver chains for it.
A man too poor to present such an offering
   selects wood that will not rot.
He looks for a skilled craftsman
   to set up an idol that will not topple.
Do you not know?
   Have you not heard?
Has it not been told you from the beginning?
   Have you not understood since the earth was founded?
He sits enthroned above the circle of the earth,
   and its people are like grasshoppers.
He stretches out the heavens like a canopy,
   and spreads them out like a tent to live in.

—ISAIAH 40:15, 17–22

One of the pitfalls of living in our troublesome world is that we can become problem- centered rather than God-centered. When this happens, we lose the proper perspective. Gradually, all our problems begin to look huge, and the strength of almighty God seems small. Instead of moving mountains by faith, we become constant worriers, creating mountains of needless pressure for ourselves and others.

Isaiah 40 is an effective prescription for those of us whose God seems small. God reminds us that He is much bigger than the world He created. He points out that compared to Him, "the nations are like a drop in a bucket" (v. 15) and the inhabitants of earth "are like grasshoppers" (v. 22). His words aren't meant to belittle us but rather to encourage us to look to Him and gain His perspective of life.

Yet God offers us more than a new perspective. He offers us something that will enable us to live by that view. If we will depend on Him instead of brooding over our problems, He will renew our strength, and wings of faith will lift our hearts above our difficulties. Some of them may be huge, but we can see them as smaller than our great God. And that makes all the difference.　　　　　　　　　　　　　—JOANIE YODER

Does Your Roof Leak?

Praise our God, O peoples,
    let the sound of his praise be heard;
he has preserved our lives
    and kept our feet from slipping.
For you, O God, tested us;
    you refined us like silver.
You brought us into prison
    and laid burdens on our backs.
You let men ride over our heads;
    we went through fire and water,
    but you brought us to a place of abundance.
I will come to your temple with burnt offerings
    and fulfill my vows to you--
vows my lips promised and my mouth spoke
    when I was in trouble.
I will sacrifice fat animals to you
    and an offering of rams;
    I will offer bulls and goats.   Selah
Come and listen, all you who fear God;
    let me tell you what he has done for me.

—PSALM 66:8–16

In a book written in 1696, I found these statements: "Sharp afflictions are to the soul as a soaking rain to the house. We know not there are such holes in the roof till the shower comes, and then we see it drop down here and there. Perhaps we did not know that there were such unmortified cuts in our soul till the storms of affliction came, then we found unbelief, impatience, and fear dropping down in many places."

How true! Affliction tests us and proves what sort of Christians we are. If there are defects in our spiritual armor, they will show up under the strain and pressure of trouble.

When the floodgates of distress are opened, it is then we echo with understanding the words of the psalmist, who exclaimed, "Save me, O God, for the waters have come up to my neck" (Psalm 69:1). Yet we need not fear, for it is our loving Father who allows the waters to come, not to drown us but to cleanse us and help us to see where our life needs repairing.

Have you been through a storm? Have you been disturbed, irritated, faithless, fearful, or rebellious? Consider that God may have put you through this difficulty to reveal your spiritual needs. By prayer, faith, and yielding to the Holy Spirit, repair the "leaky roof."   —HENRY BOSCH

Honey or Vinegar?

"Do not judge, and you will not be judged. Do not condemn, and you will not be condemned. Forgive, and you will be forgiven. Give, and it will be given to you. A good measure, pressed down, shaken together and running over, will be poured into your lap. For with the measure you use, it will be measured to you."

He also told them this parable: "Can a blind man lead a blind man? Will they not both fall into a pit? A student is not above his teacher, but everyone who is fully trained will be like his teacher.

"Why do you look at the speck of sawdust in your brother's eye and pay no attention to the plank in your own eye? How can you say to your brother, 'Brother, let me take the speck out of your eye,' when you yourself fail to see the plank in your own eye? You hypocrite, first take the plank out of your eye, and then you will see clearly to remove the speck from your brother's eye.

"No good tree bears bad fruit, nor does a bad tree bear good fruit. Each tree is recognized by its own fruit. People do not pick figs from thornbushes, or grapes from briers. The good man brings good things out of the good stored up in his heart, and the evil man brings evil things out of the evil stored up in his heart. For out of the overflow of his heart his mouth speaks."

—LUKE 6:37–45

*A*n excellent test of character is the way a person reacts under the pressure of a difficult situation. Under normal conditions most people behave in a socially acceptable manner. They give the impression that everything is under control. When they are caught off guard or are unexpectedly upset, however, they reveal their true disposition.

What is deep down inside of us will spill out when we are tested. Our reactions to pressure can reveal what we are. Jesus said, "Out of the overflow of his heart his mouth speaks" (Luke 6:45).

What comes out of your heart— honey or vinegar? When someone does something you don't like, how do you react? By maintaining your fellowship with God and relying on His Holy Spirit's guidance, what spills out of you will be pure and good.

—RICHARD DE HAAN

A Watching World

"You stiff-necked people, with uncircumcised hearts and ears! You are just like your fathers: You always resist the Holy Spirit! Was there ever a prophet your fathers did not persecute? They even killed those who predicted the coming of the Righteous One. And now you have betrayed and murdered him—you who have received the law that was put into effect through angels but have not obeyed it."

When they heard this, they were furious and gnashed their teeth at him. But Stephen, full of the Holy Spirit, looked up to heaven and saw the glory of God, and Jesus standing at the right hand of God. "Look," he said, "I see heaven open and the Son of Man standing at the right hand of God."

At this they covered their ears and, yelling at the top of their voices, they all rushed at him, dragged him out of the city and began to stone him. Meanwhile, the witnesses laid their clothes at the feet of a young man named Saul.

While they were stoning him, Stephen prayed, "Lord Jesus, receive my spirit." Then he fell on his knees and cried out, "Lord, do not hold this sin against them." When he had said this, he fell asleep.

And Saul was there, giving approval to his death.

—ACTS 7:51–8:1

We don't need ideal circumstances to be effective witnesses for Christ. Nor are God's purposes hindered by our problems.

Stephen was a powerful witness in a situation that was far from ideal. He was falsely accused and arrested (Acts 6:8–15). After he had witnessed at great length to the angry religious leaders, they rejected his words and took him out to be stoned (7:1–53).

That was the end of Stephen's witness, right? Wrong! His humble surrender to a martyr's death and his Christlike prayer that God would forgive his killers resulted in the greatest witness of Stephen's life (7:54–60).

But how does Stephen's martyrdom relate to our mundane lives? Joseph Aldrich, in his book *Life-Style Evangelism*, wrote, "When the non-Christian observes a believer responding to pressure and pain with a Spirit-controlled response, he is seeing God at work in human experience. Stephen's response to stoning caught the attention of a man named Saul!" Later, Saul became a zealous follower of Stephen's Lord (Acts 9–28).

Instead of praying for fewer difficulties so that we might witness better, let's pray that we might witness better through our difficulties. Who knows, another "Saul" may be watching.

—JOANIE YODER

Keep Your Shirt On

A gentle answer turns away wrath,
    but a harsh word stirs up anger.
The tongue of the wise commends knowledge,
    but the mouth of the fool gushes folly.
The eyes of the LORD are everywhere,
    keeping watch on the wicked and the good.
The tongue that brings healing is a tree of life,
    but a deceitful tongue crushes the spirit.
A fool spurns his father's discipline,
    but whoever heeds correction shows prudence.
The house of the righteous contains great treasure,
    but the income of the wicked brings them trouble.
The lips of the wise spread knowledge;
    not so the hearts of fools . . .
A hot-tempered man stirs up dissension,
    but a patient man calms a quarrel.

—PROVERBS 15:1–7; 18

In 1952, President Harry Truman appointed Newbold Morris to an important post. His duty was to keep a close check on crime and mismanagement in government affairs.

On one occasion, however, a Senate subcommittee called Morris to testify regarding his own New York company's sale of some ships. The interrogation became intense, and emotions ran high.

Then Morris remembered a note his wife had given him that morning. Sensing the need to calm everyone down, he called out above the clamor, "Wait a minute. I have a note here from my wife." Pulling it out of his pocket, he read the words, "Keep your shirt on." There was a burst of laughter and the tension was eased.

Whenever we are in a tension-filled situation, either with just one individual or in a group, we need to remember that "a gentle answer turns away wrath" (Proverbs 15:1). Instead of shouting angry words that only make the situation worse, we need to "keep our cool" and not "lose our head" and "fly off the handle."

Next time you encounter an angry person, "keep your shirt on" and watch the power of a gentle answer. It works!

—RICHARD DE HAAN

Tension Breaker

Rejoice in the Lord always. I will say it again: Rejoice! Let your gentleness be evident to all. The Lord is near. Do not be anxious about anything, but in everything, by prayer and petition, with thanksgiving, present your requests to God. And the peace of God, which transcends all understanding, will guard your hearts and your minds in Christ Jesus.

Finally, brothers, whatever is true, whatever is noble, whatever is right, whatever is pure, whatever is lovely, whatever is admirable—if anything is excellent or praiseworthy—think about such things. Whatever you have learned or received or heard from me, or seen in me—put it into practice. And the God of peace will be with you. —PHILIPPIANS 4:4–9

*T*ivoli Gardens, a famous amusement area in Copenhagen, Denmark, has a very unusual attraction. For a small charge, customers can try to shatter pieces of chinaware by hitting them with small wooden balls. Flawed products from area manufacturers are hung on racks at the end of the gallery, and each participant gets five chances to smash the plates, cups, saucers, and other items of china into smithereens. Touted as a great tension breaker, the activity is supposed to rid the person of unwanted anxiety.

Breaking china may be fun and may soothe frayed nerves, but the Christian has a better means of experiencing relief from tension and worry. The prophet Isaiah, addressing the Lord, declared, "You will keep him in perfect peace him whose mind is steadfast, because he trusts in you" (26:3).

We can find release from anxiety when we remember that we are always under God's watchful eye and trust Him for His protection and provision. It's reassuring to know that He is in control and that everything He allows or ordains for us is for our good.

There's nothing quite like the relaxation that comes through a deep and abiding trust in God. That's the best "tension breaker." —RICHARD DE HAAN

The Peace-filled Life

"Peace I leave with you; my peace I give you. I do not give to you as the world gives. Do not let your hearts be troubled and do not be afraid.

"You heard me say, 'I am going away and I am coming back to you.' If you loved me, you would be glad that I am going to the Father, for the Father is greater than I. I have told you now before it happens, so that when it does happen you will believe. I will not speak with you much longer, for the prince of this world is coming. He has no hold on me, but the world must learn that I love the Father and that I do exactly what my Father has commanded me. . .

"I am the true vine, and my Father is the gardener. He cuts off every branch in me that bears no fruit, while every branch that does bear fruit he prunes so that it will be even more fruitful. You are already clean because of the word I have spoken to you. Remain in me, and I will remain in you. No branch can bear fruit by itself; it must remain in the vine. Neither can you bear fruit unless you remain in me.

"I am the vine; you are the branches. If a man remains in me and I in him, he will bear much fruit; apart from me you can do nothing."

—JOHN 14:27–15:5

When H. B. Macartney, an Australian pastor, visited Hudson Taylor in China, he was amazed at the missionary's serenity in spite of his many burdens and his busy schedule. Macartney finally mustered up the courage to say, "You are occupied with millions, I with tens. Your letters are pressingly important, mine of comparatively little value. Yet I am worried and distressed while you are always calm. Tell me, what makes the difference?" Taylor replied, "I could not possibly get through the work I have to do without the peace of God which passes all understanding keeping my heart and mind." Macartney later wrote, "He was in God all the time, and God was in him. It was the true abiding spoken of in John 15."

Do you feel as if your life is more like Macartney's than Taylor's? Are you tense, troubled, anxious, fearful? Do you desire the peace Jesus promised? Then you must learn to abide in Christ as Hudson Taylor did. But you may wonder just what is meant by the expression *abiding* and how one can achieve this calmness. Abiding in Christ means to be in touch with Him continually so that the composure He experienced while on earth rules your life. You need not agonize or plead or try to work up a certain feeling. The path to abiding in Him is that of confessing and rejecting all known sin, surrendering completely, and looking trustfully to the Lord Jesus for strength. It's a continual depending on Him. You too can enjoy the serenity of a peace-filled life if you will learn to abide in Christ.

—HERB VANDER LUGT

Victory in the Kitchen

What shall we say, then? Shall we go on sinning so that grace may increase? By no means! We died to sin; how can we live in it any longer? Or don't you know that all of us who were baptized into Christ Jesus were baptized into his death? We were therefore buried with him through baptism into death in order that, just as Christ was raised from the dead through the glory of the Father, we too may live a new life.

If we have been united with him like this in his death, we will certainly also be united with him in his resurrection. For we know that our old self was crucified with him so that the body of sin might be done away with, that we should no longer be slaves to sin—because anyone who has died has been freed from sin.

Now if we died with Christ, we believe that we will also live with him. For we know that since Christ was raised from the dead, he cannot die again; death no longer has mastery over him. The death he died, he died to sin once for all; but the life he lives, he lives to God.

In the same way, count yourselves dead to sin but alive to God in Christ Jesus. Therefore do not let sin reign in your mortal body so that you obey its evil desires. —ROMANS 6:1–2

*I*f you are a Christian, you can have victory over sin. You have been released from the penalty of original sin, but you can also be free from sin's power. Not one sin or habit is strong enough to keep you in bondage.

My friend Doreen was growing in Christ, but she was oppressed by a recurring sinful practice. Whenever she was under pressure, she would let off steam by swearing at her young children. They were typical kids—noisy, arguing, making messes, and demanding attention. Her worst time was just before dinner, and her defeats usually took place in her kitchen. Doreen always confessed her sin and pleaded with the Lord to help her, but she couldn't conquer it. Then one Friday, just before the family was to leave on a holiday weekend, things were especially tense. She had a million things to do. The children were all wound up when they came home from school, and her husband was due home. Suddenly her youngsters started to fight. Just as Doreen was about to hurl some expletives, a great calm came over her. "I don't have to swear," she said. And she didn't. She experienced a great spiritual victory in the kitchen. When Doreen testified about her experience, she said that the promise of Romans 6:14—that sin should not "be [her] master"—had finally become a reality.

This can be true for every believer. So don't give up. Christ is stronger than any sin. With His help, you too can experience "victory in the kitchen." —DAVE EGNER

The Options

There was a rich man who was dressed in purple and fine linen and lived in luxury every day. At his gate was laid a beggar named Lazarus, covered with sores and longing to eat what fell from the rich man's table. Even the dogs came and licked his sores.

The time came when the beggar died and the angels carried him to Abraham's side. The rich man also died and was buried. In hell, where he was in torment, he looked up and saw Abraham far away, with Lazarus by his side. So he called to him, "Father Abraham, have pity on me and send Lazarus to dip the tip of his finger in water and cool my tongue, because I am in agony in this fire."

But Abraham replied, "Son, remember that in your lifetime you received your good things, while Lazarus received bad things, but now he is comforted here and you are in agony. And besides all this, between us and you a great chasm has been fixed, so that those who want to go from here to you cannot, nor can anyone cross over from there to us."

—LUKE 16:19–26

*L*ast time I checked, nobody likes having problems—problems with money, problems with cars, problems with computers, problems with people, problems with health. We would all prefer a life with as few difficulties as possible.

So if you were to offer people the choice between (1) a future totally free of problems, sorrow, tears, and pain, and (2) a future full of pain, suffering, regret, and anguish—they would choose option one, right?

Jesus died on the cross to give us an opportunity to experience that option. If we repent of our sins and trust Him as our Savior, He has promised us a life of fellowship with God in a place the Bible calls heaven. A place with no problems. A place where there are no more tears.

People living in a problem-filled world ought to be standing in line to grab that offer. Unfortunately, many haven't heard the good news; others have refused to trust Christ. When people die without Jesus, it's too late to take the offer, and they go to a place of torment the Bible calls hell.

Do you hate trouble and pain? Turn to Jesus and accept His offer of forgiveness. Your problems in this world won't disappear, but you'll reserve a home in heaven—a place of eternal joy and peace with God.   —DAVE BRANON

Perfect Peace Is Possible

In that day this song will be sung in the land of Judah:
We have a strong city;
God makes salvation
its walls and ramparts.
Open the gates
that the righteous nation may enter,
the nation that keeps faith.
You will keep in perfect peace
him whose mind is steadfast,
because he trusts in you.
Trust in the LORD forever,
for the LORD, the LORD, is the Rock eternal.
He humbles those who dwell on high,
he lays the lofty city low;
he levels it to the ground
and casts it down to the dust.
Feet trample it down—
the feet of the oppressed,
the footsteps of the poor.
The path of the righteous is level;
O upright One, you make the way of the righteous smooth.

—ISAIAH 26:1–7

*F*ew things (if anything at all) in this fallen world can be called perfect. But God promises to keep us in "perfect peace" if we keep our minds focused on Him and continue trusting Him (Isaiah 26:3).

So why do we find it so difficult to trust Him? Often it's because we're afraid that things won't go as we want them to unless we control them ourselves. The less we are in control, the more anxious and worried we become.

Author Hannah Whitall Smith wrote, "It is not hard, you find, to trust the management of the universe, and of all the outward creation, to the Lord. Can your case then be so much more complex and difficult than these, that you need to be anxious or troubled about His management of you?"

Yet we often think our situation is too difficult for God. If we can't solve things ourselves, we doubt that He can. We have our Christian beliefs, yes—but that isn't the same as believing God. Believing God is a personal response that grows out of our Christian faith and is expressed by our increasing trust in Him and His promises.

As our mind remains on Him, He keeps us in perfect peace. This has been the experience of countless believers, and you can experience it too.

—JOANIE YODER

Bad News?

Praise the LORD.
    Blessed is the man who fears the LORD,
    who finds great delight in his commands.
 His children will be mighty in the land;
    the generation of the upright will be blessed.
Wealth and riches are in his house,
    and his righteousness endures forever.
Even in darkness light dawns for the upright,
    for the gracious and compassionate and righteous man.
 Good will come to him who is generous and lends freely,
    who conducts his affairs with justice.
Surely he will never be shaken;
    a righteous man will be remembered forever.
He will have no fear of bad news;
    his heart is steadfast, trusting in the LORD.
His heart is secure, he will have no fear;
    in the end he will look in triumph on his foes.
He has scattered abroad his gifts to the poor,
    his righteousness endures forever;
    his horn will be lifted high in honor.
The wicked man will see and be vexed,
    he will gnash his teeth and waste away;
    the longings of the wicked will come to nothing.

—PSALM 112:1–10

Several years ago, before cell phones became common, a seminar leader asked the audience, "If someone came into this meeting, called your name, and said, 'You have a phone call,' would you assume that it was good news or bad news?" Most of us admitted we would think it was bad news, but we weren't sure why.

It points out a common burden many people carry—the fear of bad news. It may be a natural concern for the safety of those we love, but it can become an irrational dread of tragedy.

When we are most afraid, we most need confidence in God. Psalm 112 speaks of a person who fears the Lord, delights in His commandments, and is gracious to others (vv. 1, 4–5). But perhaps most striking is: "He will have no fear of bad news; his heart is steadfast, trusting in the LORD" (v. 7).

A hymn by Frances Havergal reminds us that a trusting heart is the answer for a worried mind: "Stayed upon Jehovah, hearts are fully blest; finding, as He promised, perfect peace and rest."

The Bible doesn't promise that we will never receive bad news. But it does assure us that we don't have to live each day in gnawing fear of what might happen. "His heart is secure; he will have no fear" (v. 8).   —DAVID MCCASLAND

The Jesus Way

As soon as they left the synagogue, they went with James and John to the home of Simon and Andrew. Simon's mother-in-law was in bed with a fever, and they told Jesus about her. So he went to her, took her hand and helped her up. The fever left her and she began to wait on them.

That evening after sunset the people brought to Jesus all the sick and demon-possessed. The whole town gathered at the door, and Jesus healed many who had various diseases. He also drove out many demons, but he would not let the demons speak because they knew who he was.

Very early in the morning, while it was still dark, Jesus got up, left the house and went off to a solitary place, where he prayed.   —MARK 1:29–35

Ever have one of those hectic days when you need more time than the clock offers? When everyone is after you for help and your tasks seem endless? You might wonder: Did Jesus ever struggle like this? And if so, how did He handle it?

Consider the day in Jesus' life recorded in Mark 1. It began with a visit to the synagogue to teach, which He did with authority. Then things got rough. A demon-possessed man started shouting at Jesus. Calmly but sternly the Teacher cast out the demon.

When Jesus left the synagogue, He and His friends went to Peter's house. But He couldn't rest; Peter's mother-in-law was sick and needed His healing touch. Later, the entire town gathered outside so Jesus could heal more sick people and cast out more demons. It must have been a tiring day.

How did Jesus respond? Did He take the next day off? Head for the cool mountain streams of Caesarea Philippi? No, the next day He got up before sunrise, found a solitary place, and prayed (v. 35). He sought the rejuvenating power of His Father's presence.

How do you handle a tough day? Get alone with God and seek His help. Start your day the Jesus way. —DAVE BRANON

Calm Under Pressure

This is what the Sovereign LORD, the Holy One of Israel, says:

"In repentance and rest is your salvation,
    in quietness and trust is your strength,
but you would have none of it.
You said, 'No, we will flee on horses.'
    Therefore you will flee!
You said, 'We will ride off on swift horses.'
    Therefore your pursuers will be swift!
A thousand will flee
    at the threat of one;
at the threat of five
    you will all flee away,
till you are left
    like a flagstaff on a mountaintop,
    like a banner on a hill."
Yet the LORD longs to be gracious to you;
    he rises to show you compassion.
For the LORD is a God of justice.
    Blessed are all who wait for him!

—ISAIAH 30:15–18

At the farewell for a minister who had served his church for twenty years, several preachers eloquently extolled his many virtues. One layman, however, paid a tribute that the pastor considered to be the most gratifying. He said, "I have observed him nearly every day for the past twenty years, and I've never seen him in a hurry!"

The pastor said that for years he had asked God to teach him how to renew his strength through "quietness and trust," as he had read in Isaiah 30:15. In this verse Isaiah was calling rebellious Israel to return to God and rely on Him to find new strength. The pastor, however, saw in that verse a principle applicable to his own life.

Some people are calm by nature; others are high-strung. But Christians, regardless of their temperament, can come to God in prayer and learn to renew their strength in quietness and confidence. Martin Luther said that he could get so busy that he first needed to spend at least three hours a day in prayer to get anything done. Often we reverse that order. We rush from task to task feeling flustered because we haven't taken time to be with the Lord.

Let's learn the principle set forth in Isaiah 30:15. In quietness and trust before God we find the real source of strength to stay calm.   —RICHARD DE HAAN

Peace in the Storm

Then he got into the boat and his disciples followed him. Without warning, a furious storm came up on the lake, so that the waves swept over the boat. But Jesus was sleeping. The disciples went and woke him, saying, "Lord, save us! We're going to drown!"

He replied, "You of little faith, why are you so afraid?" Then he got up and rebuked the winds and the waves, and it was completely calm.

The men were amazed and asked, "What kind of man is this? Even the winds and the waves obey him!"

—Matthew 8:23–25

During a terrible storm on the ocean, a small passenger ship rolled precariously in the roaring tempest. The furniture and anything else that could move was tied down, and the passengers were confined to their bunks for their own safety. Many on board thought the vessel was doomed.

Finally a passenger who was determined to find out if there was any hope for survival set out to see the one who was in command. Clinging to the walls and handrails, he made his way to the wave-lashed deck, up a ladder, and into the wheelhouse. He noticed that the ship was nearing land and was between some jagged rocks. It became apparent that the captain was trying to reach the safety of a calm bay up ahead. Knowing he could not make himself heard above the roar of the wind and waves, the captain just turned wordlessly to the worried passenger and smiled. Reassured, the man returned to the others and said, "Don't be afraid. All is well. I've seen the captain's face, and he smiled!"

When we are battered by the storms of life, we may be tempted to give in to feelings of hopelessness. But if we look to our sovereign Captain and commit our way to Him, we will find peace even in the midst of turmoil. We can trust Him to bring us through the storm. —Henry Bosch

About the Authors

Henry Bosch served as the first editor of the daily devotional booklet that became *Our Daily Bread* (ODB) and contributed many of the earliest articles. He was also one of the singers on the Radio Bible Class live broadcast.

Dave Branon has done freelance writing for many years and has published more than thirteen books. Dave taught English and coached basketball and baseball at the high school level before coming to RBC Ministries (RBC), where he is now the Managing Editor of *Sports Spectrum* magazine.

Dennis De Haan is a nephew of RBC founder Dr. M. R. De Haan. He pastored two churches in Iowa and Michigan before joining the RBC staff in 1971. He served as Associate Editor of ODB from 1973 until 1982 and then as Editor until June 1995. Now retired, Dennis continues editing for ODB on a part-time basis.

Mart De Haan is the grandson of RBC founder, Dr. M. R. De Haan, and the son of former president, Richard W. De Haan. Having served at RBC for over thirty years, Mart is heard regularly on the *Discover the Word* radio program and seen on *Day of Discovery* television. Mart is also a contributing writer for ODB, the Discovery Series Bible study booklets, and a monthly column on timely issues called "Been Thinking About."

Richard De Haan was President of RBC Ministries and teacher on RBC programs for twenty years. He was the son of RBC founder Dr. M. R. De Haan and wrote a number of full-length books and study booklets for RBC. Often called "the encourager," Richard was committed to faithfulness to God's Word and to integrity as a ministry. His favorite expression was "Trust in God and do the right." Richard went to be with the Lord in 2002.

Dave Egner is now retired from RBC. He was (until June 2002) Managing Editor of *Campus Journal*. He has written Discovery Series study booklets and articles for a variety of publications. Dave taught English and writing for ten years at Grand Rapids Baptist College (now Cornerstone University) before coming to RBC.

Vernon Grounds, Chancellor of Denver Seminary, has had an extensive preaching, teaching, and counseling ministry and was president of Denver Seminary. In addition to writing articles for ODB, he has also written many books and magazine articles.

David McCasland researches and helps develop biographical documentaries for *Day of Discovery* television, in addition to writing ODB articles. His books include the award-winning biography *Oswald Chambers: Abandoned to God,* a compilation of *The Complete Works of Oswald Chambers*, and *Pure Gold,* a biography of Eric Liddell.

Haddon W. Robinson is the discussion leader for the RBC Ministries' *Discover the Word* radio program, in addition to writing for *Our Daily Bread*. Dr. Robinson teaches at Gordon-Conwell Theological Seminary, where he is the Harold J. Ockenga Distinguished Professor of Preaching. He has authored several books, including *Biblical Preaching* and *Biblical Sermons,* which is currently used as a text for preaching in 120 seminaries and Bible colleges throughout the world.

David H. Roper was a pastor for more than thirty years and now directs Idaho Mountain Ministries, a retreat dedicated to the encouragement of pastoral couples. He enjoys fly-fishing, fly-tying, hiking, and just being streamside in the mountains with his wife, Carolyn. He is the author of eleven books, including *Psalm 23: The Song of a Passionate Heart.*

Paul Van Gorder began writing regularly for ODB in 1969 and continued until 1992. He also served as associate Bible teacher for the *Day of Discovery* television program and traveled extensively as a speaker for Radio Bible Class. He and his wife now live in retirement in South Carolina.

Herb Vander Lugt is Senior Research Editor for RBC Ministries and has been at RBC since 1966. In addition to ODB articles, he also writes Discovery Series booklets and reviews all study and devotional materials. Herb has pastored six churches and since retiring from the pastorate in 1989 has held three interim pastor positions.

Joanie Yoder, a favorite among ODB readers, went home to be with her Savior in 2004. She and her husband established a Christian rehabilitation center for drug addicts in England many years ago. Widowed in 1982, she learned to rely on the Lord's help and strength. She wrote with hope about true dependence on God and His life-changing power.